I0033524

If Seventy Is The New Fifty, When Do I Get To Retire?

WHY EVERYTHING YOU THOUGHT YOU KNEW
ABOUT RETIREMENT IS A LIE – AND WHAT
YOU CAN DO ABOUT IT!

Dennis Hall

Copyright © 2020 by Dennis Hall.

All rights reserved. No part of this publication may be reproduced, distributed or transmitted in any form or by any means, including photocopying, record-ing, or other electronic or mechanical methods, without the prior written per-mission of the publisher, except in the case of brief quotations embodied in critical reviews and certain other noncommercial uses permitted by copyright law. For permission requests, write to the publisher, addressed "Attention: Per-missions Coordinator," at the address below.

Dennis Hall C/- Intertype
Unit 45, 125 Highbury Road
BURWOOD VIC 3125
www.intertype.com.au

Book Layout ©2020 Intertype Publish and Print

Ordering Information:
Quantity sales. Special discounts are available on quantity purchases by cor-porations, associations, and others. For details, contact the "Special Sales De-partment" at the address above.

If Seventy Is The New Fifty, When Do I get To Retire? by Dennis Hall
ISBN 978-0-6488714-8-4

Contents

Dedicated to my brother Ken who left us far too early for a retirement in heaven

If you want to be successful, it's just this simple. Know what you are doing. Love what you are doing. And believe in what you are doing.

—Will Rogers

FORWARD

I have a magnificent library of over 3,000 books. I can assure you Dennis Hall's book will sit in a favourite place. As you journey through this book, you'll realize that this is a 'thrilling' read, it's also one of the few books that will give you a spiritually enlightened look on life. Dennis gives a new insight on the definition of true wealth, along with the inspiration to go after it.

Dennis Hall's book is a beautiful and inspirational example of 'passion in action'. If you have not yet discovered what your passion is, or how it could be possible for you to pursue it, then this book will be a magnificent resource. Read it, absorb it, and burst out of any of your "mind imposed" limits.

Nik Halik
5 Day Weekend Founder
Wall Street Journal Best Seller

Why Buy This Book?

You have picked up my book and read the blurb on the back cover and thought "Interesting…" but right now you are still wondering if this book is for you – can it really help you change your life? Can it really help you have a secure, fulfilling and rewarding retirement lifestyle?

You are likely reading this preface to help you make up your mind about buying the book, before you part with your hard-earned money. I know that because it is what I do before I purchase any self-help or personal development publication.

Let's face it – there is no shortage of books on the bookshop shelves (or Amazon catalogue!) claiming that you simply must buy a copy to be happy or successful or rich or liked or…. whatever the claim may be!

Can my book help you?

Well, only you can be the judge of that in the final analysis; but let me ask you this, do you want to be a part of the poverty economy or the prosperity economy?

To be a part of the latter you are going to need to become more proactive with your life decisions and escape the reactive mode that most people endure – and that is where this book will help you, as it provides you with a proven methodology to live a productive and enjoyable life for as long as your health will allow - as opposed to the present system where you can only achieve that for as long as your financial resources will allow!

The book is not about getting rich and it is certainly not a silver bullet, but it is about enabling you to exercise more control over your life, so that your latter years can be enjoyed without high levels of stress and worry. In fact, should you wish it, this book can show you how you can enter this phase of your life sooner than you probably thought!

Why wait until you are sixty-five (or older) to enjoy leading the life of your dreams? If you were already living that life, you would not be reading this preface!

If your retirement horizon is a little closer than you realised and you are more than a little concerned for your future and your ability to continue to provide for a decent lifestyle for yourself and your family, this book will show you how you can make changes to your life that will provide you with a more secure future – a future where you can decide what "retirement" means for you and when you want to take that step.

Then again, you may have been forced into a position where, through no fault of your own, you find your world has been turned upside down because the career you thought would take you through to retirement has come to a screeching halt – thanks to Covid19 or because your employer has had to totally rework their business model and you no longer feature in those plans.

If either sounds even remotely relevant then you should put your hand in your pocket and buy a copy – maybe even two or three, so some of your friends can ride along with you!

What Others Say About The Book

I've built 30+ successful businesses over a 35year period, one of them exceeding $130million in annual revenue. I've coached and mentored over 3000 individual business owners globally and have shared the stage with some of the greatest thought leaders of our time.

Dennis Hall is without a doubt one of the worlds quiet achievers. I've had the pleasure of knowing Dennis on both a professional and personal level and what you see is what you get. He has integrity at the highest level, and not only does he have a wealth of knowledge and a ton of experience, he is extremely humble as he engages at a level where he genuinely cares about the people he's connected to, be it on a personal or professional level, he's the real deal.

The wisdom in this book comes from his years of being on the frontline, where he's rolled up his sleeves and done all the heavy lifting and experienced first hand what the world dishes out to our society every single day. If "Seventy Is The New Fifty, When Do I Get To Retire?", is not just another book, this is 50 years of wisdom, knowledge and experience broken down into bite size chunks where you can take the lessons and implement them into your own life so you can achieve the success that you truly deserve.

Dennis Hall is an incredible individual with many wonderful qualities. He is a kind and caring father to his three amazing children, and a loving husband to his beautiful wife Iris.

If there were more people like Dennis Hall in the world, the world would be a much better place.

Ralph Anania
Entrepreneur

"If you are heading towards your Seventies, and yet you believe that - deep down - you are in your Fifties, then this book is for you. Full of practical processes and superb insights, it will guide you on staying inspired and indispensable in your advancing years."

Tony Ryan.
Author, Speaker, Entrepreneur.

Rarely does a book both inspire and educate you to be able to take control of your "later" life. This book has empowered me with some great tools which, in turn, has given me a blueprint for what I now know will be a happier future.

Rick Powell
Entrepreneur

I sit firmly in one of Dennis' core reader age groups and as some-one driven by vision and strategy many of the thoughts and ideas in this book really resonate with me. Especially as someone who has had, like Dennis, an incredibly fulfilling, complex and lucky life. As I now approach retirement, whatever that means, many of the questions spinning through my head at 3am most mornings are addressed in this thought provoking book.

Keith Dugdale
Best selling author of "Smarter Selling".

I've known and worked with Dennis Hall for two decades.

In my role as General Manager at the Australian Institute of Management, Dennis was our lead consultant who taught business people winning sales and marketing strategies. In my time as Partner at

Chandler Macleod, as a Principal Consultant, Dennis delivered customised leadership programs to much acclaim.

Dennis sees things differently from most of us. He has a gentle optimism which seems to always lead to success, combined with an uncanny ability to help others quickly see simplicity and solutions when complexity and difficulty may instead present. With this ability, in a 10 minute conversation over a two beers, Dennis saved me upwards of $100,000 by cutting through a complex opportunity and helped me see an elegant solution. Remarkable.

In his book, Dennis has approached the topic which is on most every baby boomers mind, that being aging and retirement. He has done so in the same way he approaches pretty much everything he does; with honesty, optimism, simplicity and clever solutions.

This book will assist those who are contemplating retirement or have recently retired. It will also be a great discussion starter for occasions such as BBQ's or Sunset drinks on board.

Shawn Ket

MTMgt, GradDipExL, BA, DipT, FAIM, MAICD

Director | CEO | Coach | Consultant | Sailor

Whenever I listen to Dennis Hall talk about life, business, relationships or retirement, I immediately sit up and take notice because he always makes logical sense. And when I say "always" I really mean it.

His new book "If Seventy Is The New Fifty, When Do I Get To Retire?" is a collection of the very best words and wisdoms coming straight "from brain to pen".

Dennis tells things as he sees it. He doesn't sugar coat anything. In some cases he might even offend you with his "in your face" style of writing. But when you re-read what offended you, it was probably because Dennis was hitting hard on some "home truths" which needed to be changed in your life (yes, his words probably hit a sore point or hot button).

Dennis is a great man, a loving husband to his wife Iris, and he's a pretty cool calm and collected father to his three awesome children.

I've lived with Dennis, I've worked with Dennis, and I've also had Dennis speak on my stages in workshops in Australia and Thailand (as well as quite a few keynote roles on my coaching webinars) and he's always over-delivered with tremendous educational content, action steps needed to be taken and insights into why his steps are the most logical and needed steps to be taken on your journey to success.

I'm proud to call Dennis Hall a friend, a guy who I look up to as a big brother to me and a man who I'm blessed to have in my life - he's an incredible human being we can all be educated and inspired by.

David Cavanagh

Internet Business Coach, Author, Keynote Speaker

Introduction

"It was the best of times, it was the worst of times, it was the age of wisdom, it was the age of foolishness, it was the epoch of belief, it was the epoch of incredulity, it was the season of Light, it was the season of Darkness, it was the spring of hope, it was the winter of despair, we had everything before us......"

These are the opening lines of arguably the world's bestselling historical novel, "A Tale of Two Cities" by Charles Dickens – first published in 1859. Yet those opening words have more than a passing relevance to our own, modern, world over one hundred and sixty years later.

Why? Surely, after more than 160 years, our society has long since moved on past the concerns of the mid nineteenth century.

Well, yes and no.

It turns out that our modern world has a lot in common with the mid nineteenth century. To set the scene, in 1850 the world had just come through the industrial revolution, which had started in Great Britain in the 1760's and spread around the western world through to the 1840's. This period of history is widely recognised as bringing about some of the most dramatic changes to the fabric of society since the discovery of fire, the wheel & the development of the printing press!

From 1850 – 1870 transport & communication innovations – such as steamships (from sail), railways (from horse & cart) and telegraph (from letters/snail mail), rocked the very foundations of society and, whilst they each had enormous advantages, they brought with them significant issues that had to be dealt with.

There are a lot more examples I could detail here but I won't as it would result in this introduction extending to more than half of the book - but I will mention some of them as the book unfolds.

Here we are in the early part of the twenty first century and we are still trying to deal with the ongoing impacts of technology. There's hardly any element of our modern-day society that hasn't been impacted by the ever increasing pace of technological innovations – and those impacts have both an upside and a downside.

Just ask a Taxi driver what they think of Uber (& other ride sharing "Apps") or a motel owner what they think of AirBnB. Indeed, entire industries have been decimated by the introduction of technological advancements – Kodak, once a giant in the photographic industry, filed for bankruptcy in 2012. Blockbuster video ceased operations in 2010. The list of victims is long and contains more than a few illustrious names – proving that no organisation, no matter what its size, is immune from the march of progress.

We are all living through some of the most tumultuous times in modern history! That's not the elephant in the room...

There is a much bigger issue staring us right in the face which will fundamentally change the entire fabric of society. In fact, the first big shots are already being fired in what promises to be a challenging battle. What is this issue?

It is the ageing of our populations. Or, put another way, the "Age wave". According to Dr Ken Dychtwald, Ph.D., who first envisioned this demographically driven transformation and coined the term, the "Age wave", this issue is already at work, reshaping social and cultural trends, marketplace opportunities, productivity, and consumption patterns.

Here's something for you to consider right now...

In the developed world – those parts of the planet where industry, education & society result in prosperity (to varying degrees), the structure of society is based around a model where the first twenty years of the life of the population are focused on development and education, which is followed by forty to forty-five years of a productive work life before retirement at around 65.

Here's where the problem lies – that model is based on a world that no longer exists!

You see that model's development had its beginnings in the late eighteenth and early nineteenth centuries – when the average life expectancy of men was around 55 years and women 59 years. This meant that, with a retirement age of 65 for men and 60 for women, society could afford to offer pensions and support for the retired population, as a large enough percentage of the population were working and the taxes, they paid could cover that expense.

After all, once you retired, you weren't expected to live too long – if you even made it that far in the first place! Meanwhile, here in the twenty first century, in developed nations around the world, the average life expectancy of men is now around 80 years and women 84 years and increasing rapidly.

Now that the Baby boomer generation (those born between 1945-1964) is reaching retirement age, there are more people retiring than there are entering the workforce – and those retiring are likely to live for at least twenty years after they retire.

Due to this, society is struggling to fund the ballooning cost of supporting an ageing population – not just in terms of pensions but also with health and other associated costs. Add to that the impact of technological advances and you have a potentially catastrophic cocktail that we must start to deal with. That brings us to the purpose of this book.

With the average person now expected to experience twenty or more years as a "Retiree" we must start to rethink what retirement means.

Personally, I am not one to advocate that people simply remain in the workplace longer, as that approach creates as many problems as it solves. However, I do believe that we are all capable of reshaping our lives in order to live a more productive and fulfilling life in what many consider to be the "Twilight" of their lives.

If you are reading this book it is highly likely that you are over fifty years old and that retirement is becoming more than some far off concept – it is looming closer & you are wondering what it will mean for you.

You are likely to be in one of five categories:

1. You are somewhere between five to fifteen years away from the retirement age and have started to consider what retirement might look like. Your views on retirement are likely positive and you are happy at the thought of being able to put up your feet. You also probably believe that you are largely "On track" for a successful retirement.

2. Retirement is around five years away for you. You are becoming excited at the prospect of being able to take it easy and are looking forward to all the recreational activities you have imagined for yourself. This feeling of excitement is somewhat tempered by nagging concerns as to whether your superannuation is enough to fund this new lifestyle.

3. You have just retired or will do so in the next few months. There's a feeling of relief and exhilaration – now you get to live the dream! Enjoy the feeling while it lasts. Unfortunately, for most of us, this "Honeymoon" period only lasts for about twelve months!

4. You have been retired for between one to twelve years and reality has well and truly bitten! You are no longer sure about who you really are and where you fit in. You have growing concerns around your health and financial wellbeing. You miss the interaction you had with former work colleagues and you feel a lack of engagement with the world at large.

5. You have been retired for over twelve years. You are struggling with coming to terms with what your life was

all about. You have anxiety issues concerning the cost of living and feel sadness over the passing of friends and family members. Thoughts about your legacy become more frequent. Spirituality becomes more important.

No matter how "amazing" your retirement years seem or are for you, you are going to go through these stages – Dr Ken Dychtwald's research into thousands of retirees confirms this for us. This book is all about showing you how you can exercise more control over this stage of your life's journey – without a reliance on government handouts and without having to sacrifice all the things that you enjoy about your present lifestyle. Contrary to what far too many people believe, we do live in the "Best of times" …. an age of wisdom, an age of foolishness, it is the epoch of belief, but also the epoch of incredulity, it is the season of Light, it is the spring of hope, you have everything before you.

The question is, what are you going to do with it? Hopefully, this book will help you to decide about that. I have broken the book down into three broad sections;

Section One is all about setting the tone, taking a snapshot of the world we now live in, exploring possibilities and a look at my story to date – which I am hoping that you can utilise as a case study, a "Proof of concept" if you like, which demonstrates that you can make changes to your life that, currently, you may think are outside the realms of possibility for you. I believe that this section will start you on a bit of "blue sky thinking" for yourself – to start you thinking about possibilities for your future and the sort of life you could be living in your latter years.

Section Two is where I start to provide you with the details you will need in order to make the changes to your current situation without having to tip the "baby out with the bath water."

Be warned, you are going to have to prepare yourself to make some massive leaps in your thinking if you are going to enjoy the sort of lifestyle you may well deserve but that few people actually experience. This section of the book is going to require you not just to shift your thinking but also to "roll up your sleeves" as you work through what is a substantial amount of detailed content. It will show you how to plan your journey, as well as what you can expect & what hurdles you are likely to face (with ideas on how to deal with them).

Section Three is all about putting your plan into action! Here's where you can really benefit from my experiences – no plan survives intact once it is activated, so here I also deal with how to cope with the unexpected and where your biggest challenges are going to come from.

Each section is crammed full of tools, techniques, processes and systems designed to assist you on your journey towards your new lifestyle. There are also numerous references for additional support resources on the book's support website (www.whencaniretire.com.au). In short, in reading this book you will have everything you are likely to need to make your journey possible.

The best part of all of this is that I know, from first-hand experience and observation, that these tools, techniques, processes and systems all work because I have used them (to varying degrees) to achieve my own chosen lifestyle.

This book is not a collection of theories – my own journey is testament to what I am going to be sharing with you and, whilst my circumstances will be different to yours, I can assure you that, if you follow in my footsteps, you too can enjoy a lifestyle of your choosing rather than one that is forced upon you.

Let's get started!

A World Of Endless Possibilities

"Man, often becomes what he believes himself to be. If I keep on saying to myself that I cannot do a certain thing, it is possible that I may end by really becoming incapable of doing it. On the contrary, if I have the belief that I can do it, I shall surely acquire the capacity to do it even if I may not have it at the beginning."
Mahatma Gandhi

This first part of the book (and your journey) is all about setting the tone for the rest of what is to come. We will be starting with a look at how our own thinking in today's changing world works against us and that this thinking is one of the first things we need to address if we are going to achieve the sort of success we are seeking. Then, I will share with you my journey, what led me to where I am now and, importantly, how I got here. It's important for you to understand that I have made the journey you are contemplating right now.

We are also going to be examining success and work towards a definition that represents your desires, dreams and hopes, rather than a set of numbers in a bank account or a street address. You will need to become a more independent thinker as your journey unfolds and so we will explore mindset and how to develop a mindset that works for you and with you as opposed to sabotaging your every move.

Engaging in the right sort of thinking is not easy and most people simply give in to external influences and end up just "Going with the flow". If you are going to be able to prevent this from happening to you, then you are going to have to be passionate about creating the sort of life you have imagined for yourself – so we will also be looking at how to identify just what you are passionate about.

Passion creates energy and enthusiasm and you are going to need that in spades to keep your momentum going!

It's not all upside here. You can be certain that your journey will be fraught with risk. So, we will also be discussing risk – how to identify it and how to deal with it. Risk is a part of everyday life. Some risks you can eliminate but you cannot eliminate all risk – so you need to find ways you can go about managing it.

Make no mistake, whether you move forward or stay where you are – there is risk involved. Staying put, not making changes, going with the "Flow" may seem like a safe option but you are still taking a risk - what if it is not as safe as you thought?

I'm sure many people at the beginning of 2020 would have thought that they were secure in their current position – why take a risk when things are going well? But then, BANG! Covid19 came at us from left field and staying where we were was not so attractive anymore.

Then there are those companies no longer in existence – they all decided to minimise their risks by staying put and focusing on what they knew best, rather than taking a chance and moving forward. The result was that the world passed them by. I'm hoping that this book will reduce the chances of that happening to you, provided you do something with the information the book contains!

We will end section one with an expose on all of those "Naysayers" who are going to look you in the eye and tell you that you are crazy, that your plan will never work, so don't even try.

Let's start the journey. I'm ready if you are!

Yesterday's Thinking In Today's World

"We cannot solve our problems with the same thinking we used when we created them."
Albert Einstein

There are two key areas of influence shaping the twenty first century – one is technology and the other is societal expectation. Let's first explore technology.

Technology As A Driver For Change

We have just entered the third decade of the twenty first century – this is not the realm of science fiction, yet many of the science fiction programs we were exposed to as children situated their characters and storylines in precisely the time period in which we currently live!

Unfortunately, the mainstream population is not prepared for the world we inhabit – primarily because their thinking is based upon a world that no longer exists. Let me explain.

During the first fifty years of the twentieth century, society went through some massive changes, many of these were borne out of nineteenth century thinking such as locomotives and rail networks, steam ships, the telegraph, radio transmission, distributed electricity networks, motorised vehicles etc. These provided significant impetus for growth and prosperity – but this was hampered by two world wars and the Wall Street crash of the nineteen twenties.

Post-World War II, the western world has enjoyed unparalleled prosperity with only a few minor bumps in the road. During that post war period we have also moved from a position where the availability of resources determined a country's wealth, to a position where the utilisation of resources drives wealth.

In the second half of the twentieth century we have seen entire industries come and go, companies that were household names have since been almost forgotten. Fast forward to the twenty first century and technology has accelerated to dizzying speeds. In fact, predicting what happens from here is pretty much impossible! It's like going back to the late nineteenth century and forecasting that the birth of electricity would result in the development of computers. The fact is, we do not know what technology is going to bring us - other than change and on an unprecedented scale.

Here we are in the "roaring twenties" of the twenty first century and we have a situation where;

- The world's largest retailer has no stores (Amazon)
- The world's largest accommodation provider owns no hotels (AirBnB)
- The world's largest B2B wholesaler has no physical showrooms (Alibaba)
- The world's largest vehicle ride provider owns no vehicles (Uber)
- The world's largest music/video provider has no studios (iTunes)

Retail giants are downsizing or disappearing as consumers exercise the choice that the internet provides them with, and manufacturers continue to amalgamate and relocate (often internationally) in order to remain economically viable.

Global communication is now commonplace, and we think nothing of picking up our smartphone to make a call to someone on the other side of the world. Thanks to the internet and satellite technologies, we can have meetings via video connections that involve people from multiple countries, without ever leaving our homes!

When I returned to Australia in 1975 I had to book in advance with the telephone company (there was only one) any calls I wanted to make at busy periods (like Easter and Christmas) to my family and friends in England and I could only stay on the line for a maximum 30 minutes (the quality of the call was often poor to boot).

We can travel halfway around the world in less than twenty-four hours, at extremely affordable cost – we live in amazing times! The world as it was fifty years ago no longer exists – but we are still trying to apply twentieth century thinking to this new world environment. Which is why every prediction you are likely to read about the future of work will be wrong.

This is why Futurists often err in their predictions – they use current thinking and project forward, whereas the really good ones try to project their thinking forward as well.

In the late nineteen sixties the world population was a little over three billion people and there was a real concern that if population growth continued at past rates (approx. plus seven hundred million people per decade), we would not be able grow enough food to feed everyone and mass starvation would occur. This was not a concern voiced by a few crackpots but by many University educated professionals. Yet, here we are, sixty years later, in the roaring twenties of a new century, with a global population of over seven billion (still growing by around seven hundred million people per decade) and those forecasts have not come to pass.

Certainly, there are areas of the world where starvation is happening but that is not due to an inability to produce food. Those areas where starvation is a part of life are regions where political instability and armed conflict is rife and food is being used as a weapon.

Why didn't those predictions of global mass starvation come to pass? Simply because of flawed thinking (these days we call it "Modelling"). The alarmists and futurists (not all but many) simply added population growth projections and compared those to the then current food production capacities and saw that, based on this, we weren't producing enough food to cope with population growth.

What they did not allow for was the impact of technology in making our food production more efficient and the advances in storage and transportation facilities to get the food from where it was produced to where it was needed. This is one of the reasons I smile when I see stories in the media about how technology is going to destroy all jobs. While the debate about the future of work continues to get plenty of media coverage, much of it is of the alarmist "the robots are coming to take your job" version. It makes for good press and interesting, populist stories – but is only looking at a small part of a much bigger picture.

However, that is not to say that in the future jobs will not be lost to automation and technology because they will. The real question is not what jobs will be lost but what jobs will be created?

While machine learning, artificial intelligence and robotic process automation will make a difference to which jobs survive and how work is done. There are two other factors — lengthening human lifespans and changes in society — that will have bigger impacts. We will be exploring both shortly.

What we are facing is nothing new - It is part of a continuum that has often predicted an apocalyptic future but rarely delivered one. Over the last 50-years we have moved, in Australia, from a position where twice as many men worked as women, to one where that gap hovers around 15%. The rest of the developed world is similar.

We have moved from a world where work was largely done by men, in special places built for work and at prescribed times of day, to one where work is open to almost anyone, often done anywhere, and where people are 'on' most of the time. While the journey to full equality is far from done yet — there are still fewer women in the workforce, fewer women in senior roles, significantly more women in part-time roles, and pay inequality is still a work in progress — we are well down this track.

As these remaining issues are resolved, society will also continue to change its views on other issues such as acceptable working hours, employment versus contracting, careers as against jobs, the role of older workers (of whom there will be many more), the responsibilities of employers and corporations and so on. This will happen irrespective of technology changes — but technology will play an important role in enabling and allowing these changes.

One of the current trends in the future of work debate is to analyse the impact of new technology on jobs, counting the likely damage that automation will cause. Let us take satellite navigation (Satnav) as an example:

At first glance, the immediate implications of Satnav would have been that a small proportion of a taxi driver's role would be replaced: the requirement to know how to get from A to B.

Not enough of the role changed to replace the taxi driver, despite this 'robotic augmentation' you still needed one taxi driver per taxi. On that maths, one would have thought taxi driver jobs would be safe from the impact of automation until self-driving vehicles became a reality.

However, the Satnav also enabled a whole new business model: Uber and other ride-sharing apps. Anyone who has used Uber knows most drivers would be lost, literally, without their GPS-enabled app.

Uber was at the forefront of a new economy of gig workers — with multiple jobs, no career paths, the opportunity to be entrepreneurial, no age restrictions and so on. In the meantime, while taxis were threatened, they also upped their game in both service, technology and customer service. Whilst Taxi drivers would prefer Uber and other ride share businesses not exist, a balance between the two has developed. So, whilst there may be fewer Taxi Drivers, there are a lot of ride share drivers – the net job loss is negligible.

The same story of apparent destruction but actual creation could be told for many technologies. Wi-Fi, an Australian invention, for example, enabled café working culture and spawned activity-based working.

Blockchain (on which Bitcoin is based) probably won't lead to a cryptocurrency revolution and the end of banks but it might very well spin off any number of new opportunities where we need secure, transparent transaction records.

The lesson here is that we really don't know where new technology is going to take us and just 'counting' the impact on the existing scenario and assuming the worst is only a small part of the picture, while the bigger cause and effect on society is harder to predict. What is an absolute truth is that every time technology or society changes, it creates disruption and that impact is a two-sided coin – on the one side there is displacement of what is currently in place, be that jobs, careers or organisations. However, on the other side lies opportunity – steam engines replaced horse drawn carts and sailing ships, but those engines required both building and servicing as well as a myriad of support mechanisms (such as railway tracks and stations, port upgrades and dry docks).

If we don't know precisely what the future is going to look like, which jobs will survive and which new ones will be invented, what should you do in the meantime as society waits for this world to unfold? How do we take control of the future by acting now? Here are some examples where disruption is likely to hit hard over the next five to seven years:

1. The Post Office

Get ready to imagine a world without the post office. The economic model the business was built on no longer exists – Email has destroyed their main income producer which was letters. Couriers such as Fed Ex, and UPS have significantly eroded their parcel income base. Most of your mail every day is junk mail and bills – even these are decreasing (as, unfortunately, email spam increases).

2. Retail Banking

When was the last time you wrote a cheque? It costs the financial system billions of dollars a year to process cheques. Plastic cards and online transactions will lead to the eventual demise of the cheque. How often do you even visit a local branch (as opposed to using an ATM)?

3. The Newspaper

Emerging generations simply don't read the newspaper. As I discovered myself when having to explain to a twenty something what the term "Comic strip" meant (their interpretation was NSFW - Not Suitable For Work)! They certainly don't subscribe to a daily delivered print edition. It will go the way of the milkman and the laundry man. The rise in mobile Internet devices and e-readers has caused all the newspaper and magazine publishers to form an alliance. They have met with Apple, Amazon, and the major mobile phone carriers to develop a model for paid subscription services – but is that the answer when there are so many free news distribution services out there?

4.   The Book

You say you will never give up the physical book you hold in your hand and turn the literal pages. I said the same thing about downloading music from iTunes. I wanted my hard copy CD. But I quickly changed my mind when I discovered I could get albums for half the price without ever leaving home to get the latest music. The same thing is now happening with books.

You can browse a bookstore online and even read a preview chapter before you buy - and the price is less than half of a physical book, as well as the convenience (you didn't have to leave home to buy it, nor did you have to wait for delivery) Will books disappear? That is both a contentious and emotive question, after all you are reading this! Make no mistake though, the book industry is enduring massive disruption – change is here.

5.   The Land Line Telephone

Do you even need a land line phone anymore? Most people keep it simply because they've always had it; but you are paying double charges for the extra service. All the mobile phone companies will let you call customers using the same provider for no charge against your minutes – depending on your usage plan.

6.   Music

The music industry is undergoing massive disruption - not just because of illegal downloading. It's the lack of innovative new music being given a chance to get to the people who would like to hear it. The problem is the record labels and the radio conglomerates who are desperately trying to retain their past power. Over 40% of the music purchased today is "catalogue items," meaning traditional music the public is familiar with, older established artists. This is also true on the live concert circuit. The industry is going to look very different in five years but one thing that will not change is people's need to be entertained and that's where opportunities are going to come from.

To explore this fascinating and disturbing topic further, check out the book, *"Appetite for Self-Destruction"* by *Steve Knopper*, and the video documentary, *"Before the Music Dies."* and *"The Long Tail"* by *Chris Anderson* is also a great read in this space.

7. Television

Revenues to the networks are down dramatically. Not just because of the economy. People are watching TV and movies streamed from their computers. And they're playing games and doing lots of other things to take up the time usually spent watching TV. Prime time shows have degenerated down to lower than the lowest common denominator.

Networks have brought this on themselves, in a similar way that the music industry did. For decades the big players decided what we could watch and when, but that power has been destroyed by digital technologies. They seem content to focus on "reality" programming, but this is fast reaching saturation point.

We now have more choice as to what we watch and when and the public is exercising that choice. What is happening is that the power is shifting from the content producers and distributors to the public. Massive changes in this space are already surfacing but even more is to come. Here's where our thinking needs to change – with the previous seven examples it is easy to focus on what has been lost or displaced. What we should be doing though is focusing on the opportunity that has (or soon will be) created in its place.

I would encourage you to do just that – grab a piece of paper, have a look at those examples (or come up with some additional ones of your own – there are plenty when you think about it!) and identify some opportunities that the disruption could create. It is this "Opportunity" space that will show you where you need to be if you are going to start controlling what happens to you as opposed to allowing others to exercise that control.

The Gig Economy

Here is an example of opportunity that is delivered by technology. The Gig Economy gets its name from each piece of work being akin to an individual 'gig' – a music industry term for an individual concert or paid performance -although, such work can fall under multiple names.

The rapid growth in the Gig Economy has moved it from being a fad to a trend and suggests that this is one of the pathways for the future of work. Perhaps not all work but certainly a healthy slice. Whilst not all work in the Gig economy utilises technology platforms, many do. Names like Airtasker, Freelancer, Uber Eats, Menu Log, Fiverr – even AirBnB and Uber are all examples of the rise in popularity of the Gig Economy

Working in the Gig Economy requires a shift in mindset for those seeking to make their living from it. If you are expecting to feel secure within the Gig Economy you must develop a stronger self-image of your worth, value & ability than you had when you had a "job".

There's a great article on "The Pros And Cons Of The Gig Economy" in the resources section of the support website (www.whencaniretire.com.au).

Unfortunately, our education system is letting us down here– instead of preparing our children for this new world by teaching critical thinking skills, education institutions are still heavily knowledge based. By that I mean that our children are not taught to think but to remember.

That methodology was adequate when humankind's knowledge was relatively static, but in an age where new discoveries are accelerating it is no longer possible to remember everything. It is estimated that humankind's knowledge is doubling every eighteen months – we simply cannot hope to remember everything anymore. Instead, we must know where to source the information we need and, importantly, what questions to ask in order that the right answers can be arrived at. This is the basis of critical thinking.

This is why Google has been so successful – ask the right question of Google and you will have no shortage of information to access to arrive at an answer. We are also being let down by the mainstream media who seem to have forgotten the important role they play in the distribution of information. Instead, the big players in our present media environment seem obsessed with who can deliver the most outrageous headline and their bias and distortion of facts has become so blatant that many people question their relevance.

Thankfully, the internet provides us all with access to a variety of information sources, data and viewpoints – none of which is of much use unless you apply some critical thinking. Simply accepting one media outlet's view over another without question or further investigation is not going to lead you to informed decision making.

Societal Dynamics As A Driver For Change

Whilst advances in technology are acting as catalysts for change in our society, this is not the only force in play. Societal dynamics are also a key driver for change - the trends for ageing and life expectancy. At the turn of the twentieth century the average life expectancy for males in Australia was fifty-five years and for females fifty-nine years.

This had changed dramatically by the turn of the twenty first century to seventy-nine years for males and eighty-three years for females. That is a very healthy (pun intended!) increase!

As of 2020 that has increased further, to a little over eighty years for males and eighty-four years for females and is forecast to continue to climb upwards for the foreseeable future.

The reasons for the increases lie in three main categories:

1. Improvements in living conditions in the early 20th century, such as better water supplies, sewerage systems, food quality and health education, etc
2. Improving social conditions and advances in medical technology such as mass immunisation and antibiotics.

3. Lower infant mortality.

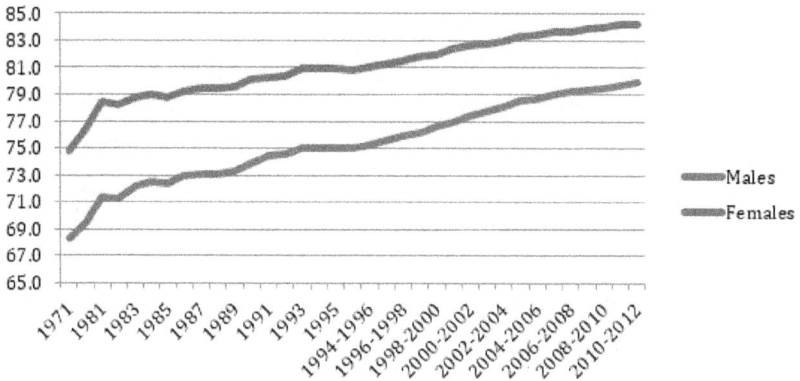

Figure 1: Australian Life Expectancy Chart

Increased life expectancy is a good thing, but it does come with some issues that we are going to have to deal with – and soon. Here's why….

We are at the start of a "Longevity revolution" which is also being referred to as the "Age Wave" (a term coined by Dr Ken Dychtwald – search for him on YouTube, he has some interesting ideas). For more than fifty thousand years humankind has been used to an environment where life expectancy was around the fifty to sixty-five year mark. Live longer than that and you were considered to have enjoyed a very good life.

However, today that expectancy is now over eighty. In fact, two thirds of all the people in mankind's history, who have lived to over sixty five, are alive today! This has impacts in just about every aspect of society;

- Family life
- Social life
- Working life

Clearly, living longer is very desirable. However, it does have some significant implications – both socially and economically.

Social implications include:

- Perceptions of what being "Old" is starting to be challenged

- As we, ourselves, age our ideas as to where we fit into society start to change
- Society's expectations of its aged population start to shift
- Areas of divergence between generations become more acute (i.e.; "OK Boomer" as a term to shut down older members of society by younger members of society)

Economic implications include:

- Re-examining an appropriate retirement age
- Funding the health and social services provided to older citizens
- Determining the role(s) older citizens can play in the workforce
- Increasing aged care infrastructure (i.e.; hospitals, dwellings, transport, etc) as the aged population increases

The above are, by no means, the only implications but they are the main ones and a few of these we will discuss here. I should stress, though, that it is not the purpose of this book to suggest solutions for these and other, related issues. This book is focused on providing individuals, like yourself, with some "Food for thought" and with some strategies, processes and systems that will allow you to make more informed decisions and choices as to what to do in your circumstances. More on those later. For now, we are going to discuss some of these economic and social implications in a little more detail.

Let's begin that discussion with the term "Retirement". The formal definition of that term and the one that is currently widely supported in the community is "a withdrawal from one's position or occupation or from active working life". For the bulk of the population "retirement" is when you sit back and take it easy. It's when you will get to do all those things that you couldn't do (but wanted to) whilst work and other commitments got in the way. Is that what this phase of our lives is about? To answer that question, we need to track back a little.

In Australia (and much of the western world) the retirement age of sixty five years for men and sixty years for women was established in 1909 - a time when the average life expectancy was fifty five and fifty nine years respectively. Basically, not many people were expected to qualify for a pension! Even when, in the middle part of the twentieth century, life expectancy increased to seventy years for men and seventy three years for women, retirement only lasted for five to nine years and there were enough people in the workforce (paying taxes) to support that increased cost.

The picture is very different in the 2020's. Not only has life expectancy increased to a little over eighty years for males and eighty four years for females (and is forecast to continue to climb upwards for the foreseeable future), but the number of people retiring is now exceeding the number of people entering the workforce.

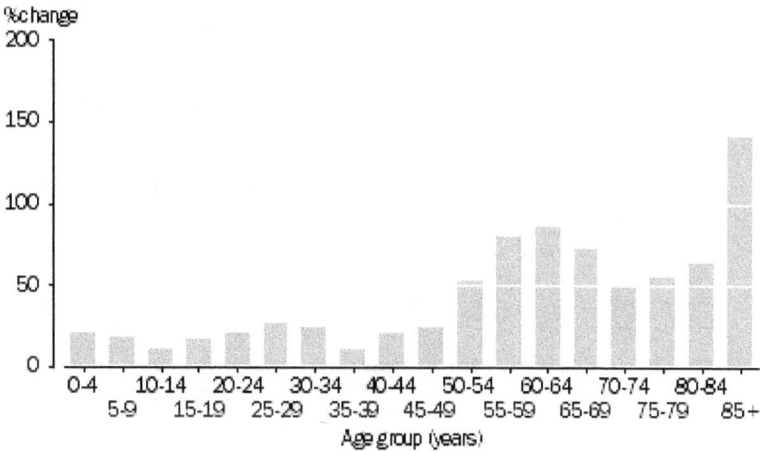

Figure 2: Australia's Ageing Population

As of 2015 there were more than 1.6 billion people aged 50+, with this demographic predicted to double in numbers by 2050. In Australia we have one of the longest expectations of lifespan populations in the world. As great as that is, it does present us with some challenges (and we are not alone with these!)

We are faced with a situation where our ageing population's needs can no longer be funded using the model that all of us have been brought up with – this is one of the reasons why successive governments have pushed ahead with increasing the retirement age.

This does not solve the problem, it merely delays the crunch time when the system collapses – unless something is done to address the core issues (again, not a topic for this book). After all, whether you retire at sixty five, sixty seven or even seventy, there is still a growing period to deal with (at this stage a minimum of ten years but rising fast) where the social system is required to support its elderly citizens.

The fact that people retiring are going to be around for more than twenty years also significantly alters their perceptions as to what to do. Just how many TV shows can you watch, and trips can you make over a twenty to twenty five year period before you get bored or run out of money? (or both!) We (as a society) need to re-evaluate not just retirement but the whole life journey continuum that has been entrenched for millennia but has especially been reinforced over the last century or two.

Figure three compares what that life journey may look like.

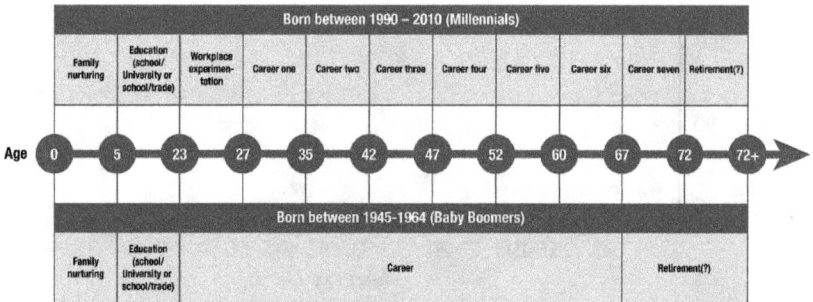

Figure 3: Life Journey Continuum

Obviously, in relation to Millennials, the above is a prediction not an actuality (yet). However, no matter how the continuum ends up, you can be certain that it will be different from what we have been used to – it must be. The world we have grown up believing to be there is, in fact, not there at all!

Job security is no longer a given – no matter who your employer is. Social security benefits can no longer be relied upon as they once were.

Both economic and social drivers are changing – the continuum has to change with these, and we are already seeing signs of this. Talk with any Millennial in the workplace and they will tell you that they do not expect their current job/career to last. Further, they expect to have to continually learn and update their skills in order to remain relevant. Boomers find this hard to understand because their world was different to this one.

No matter what generation you are from (I'm a Boomer myself), we are all living in the same world. We simply need to learn to adapt to that and the people who do (and I am hoping that you are one) are the ones who will continue to enjoy all the possibilities that this new world represents.

Before we leave this topic, here are a few things for you to consider:

- What do you plan to do with the longevity bonus that you have been gifted? If you are male and reading this it is likely that you will have at least twenty years of "Retirement" to enjoy. If you are female, you will have at least twenty two years of "Retirement" to enjoy – what will you do with this?
- Currently, our society largely holds the belief that education is for the young. However, with more than twenty years at your disposal, is that belief still valid?
- There is no shortage of advice available for students to base sound educational decisions around (especially at a tertiary level). There is also no shortage of careers advice – but there is practically nothing on how to gainfully utilise your longevity bonus (outside of hard financial/investment matters). What can/should be done about this?
- If the government cannot sustain financially supporting its aged population what are you going to do about that?

Clearly, we need to redefine what this "retirement" term means. For society that is going to take time but you, as an individual, can redefine the term for yourself – in no time at all!

Retirement is not just about;

- Trying to stay young – you are not young, but you are not old either!
- Watching more TV or listening to more music
- Taking more trips
- Becoming a de-facto babysitter (although grandchildren are a great source of joy)

For me, I look at "retirement" as an opportunity. As you progress through this book, I am hoping that you will come to share that definition with me.

Retirement is about;

- Starting a new chapter in your life – one that you can write yourself!
- Relationships – rekindling old ones/exploring new ones

Learning

- Having fun – doing the things you want to do as opposed to what you had to do
- Legacy – being able to contribute to society in other ways than the work/tax model.

Depending on when you decide to "retire" you will have had anything from thirty to forty five years in the workforce being productive. Just because you enter this new phase of life does not mean that you cannot continue to contribute.

How well you adapt to this transition, and how much of a contribution you are going to be able to make, will come down to one critical success factor – your mindset. How you think will determine whether your longevity bonus will be determined as being well spent or wasted. We will certainly spend some time on the topic later.

Right now though, there is an event that has impacted everyone's mindset and that is the Covid19 Pandemic. So, before we go any further, let's explore what that event means for us.

The Covid19 Pandemic – Proof That All Plans Are Subject To Change

"Experience provides us lessons – catastrophe accelerates the process."
Dennis Hall

Throughout the course of this book I will be mentioning that you need to have plan A, B, C etc., in order that you are prepared for contingencies and nothing demonstrates the validity of this need better than Covid19.

In February 2020 I thought that I was almost finished this book – but the universe had other ideas! The emergence of Covid19 and its rapid and catastrophic spread throughout the world, has changed absolutely everything for just about everyone in the industrialised world. This situation reads like a Stephen King horror novel – only worse!

With the closure of just about every business in Australia in March 2020, lockdowns and social distancing, we have all had to re-evaluate many of the aspects of day to day life that we have, for so long, taken for granted. The rest of the industrialised world is experiencing similar conditions, so Australia is not on its own in this. Socially, we have had to remain isolated from friends and family. Travel plans have, largely, gone out the window, international travel is totally out of the question. Professionally, if your employer is still in business, work conditions have changed dramatically – from operating hours of work to working from home – even having to consider taking on different roles and responsibilities.

If you operate your own business, it is likely that you have had to significantly change your methods of operation as both government regulations and customer expectations challenge the very existence of the business. Certainly, government payments, subsidies, grants and the like are cushioning a reasonable proportion of the financial burdens people affected most by all of this would otherwise suffer. However, not everyone is receiving these and the harsh reality is that these support payments cannot continue indefinitely.

As I write this chapter of the book in August 2020, there remains significant uncertainty as to what our world is going to look like six, twelve or twenty four months from now. Victoria is experiencing a second wave of the virus, resulting in severe isolation restrictions. New South Wales is also experiencing virus outbreaks that the government is struggling to manage and New Zealanders living in Auckland have just experienced another isolation shutdown as a fresh outbreak surfaces.

Queensland, Western Australia, South Australia, Tasmania and the Northern Territory have closed their borders – New South Wales, by default, is isolated too.

Is this going to be our new normal? Will we ever be in a position to return to the world we knew at the beginning of 2020? You will be reading this book at a point beyond all of this and will, no doubt be facing other issues not prominent at the time of my writing these words. The real question though is, what can you do in such uncertain times?

Well, as it turns out, quite a bit! The whole premise of this book is based upon taking more control of your life so that, in retirement, you are not so dependent on external elements (such as government support and superannuation) and if there is one thing that this pandemic has demonstrated it is that nothing is really for certain – everything is subject to change.

You can decide whether you are just going to let the flow of circumstances push and pull you this way and that or whether you are going to make the effort to steer your own course through these currents of adversity and uncertainty.

You steer your own course by following the processes and systems detailed for you in this book – the Covid19 pandemic is just another catalyst for change – the same way that your impending retirement milestone is a catalyst, as was my wife and I's "adventure" to experience life overseas for two years - which I will be telling you about later.

Yes, the pandemic is more far reaching and impactive, but it is, nonetheless, just a catalyst - which you can use as an excuse to hold you back or as a reason to propel you forward.

For many people, Covid19 is a significant bump in the road but one from which they expect to recover reasonably well. However, there are a significant number of people whose lives will simply never be the same.

For instance, imagine that you had a career in aviation – let's say as a pilot – and you had twenty years or more of experience under your belt. Not only would you be on a very attractive salary package but you would have been looking forward to a retirement package that would make your life after aviation very comfortable indeed.

Then Covid19 hits, your industry is shut down and your employer either goes into receivership or rationalises its workforce dramatically. Now, as a pilot you are not only out of work but your career is brought to an abrupt end. Every airline in the world is facing the same conditions, so it is not a case of simply finding another airline to work for because no-one is hiring and that situation will not change for at least two more years – by which time you are in an age bracket where you are no longer considered a good hire.

What to do?

To re-enter the workforce is going to require total retraining – and that is assuming that employers will consider you (ex-pilot) as a potential employee. Ageism is rampant – older people (50 plus) are often discriminated against when it comes to hiring new staff.

So, from being in high demand you are now basically on the employment scrap heap. "Forced" into retirement – years before you were ready for it!

And that situation is repeated over and over, in industry after industry. Aviation, tourism, hospitality, manufacturing, property and business services, warehousing, conferencing and events, entertainment (concerts, live music, cinemas, etc) to name but a few.

If you are faced with this prospect these are very concerning times for you. The good news is that you can do something about it and we will be covering some of your options in Section Two.

Before we get to that, here are some critical thoughts to help you, hopefully, start your process of moving forward:

- In March 2020 Australia's unemployment rate stood at 6.22%
- As of July 2020, that figure had risen to 7.5% and is predicted to go beyond 10% as the economic impacts of the pandemic bite harder
- Ageism or discrimination against older aged workers, is one of the few areas of socially sanctioned discrimination remaining today
- Unemployed people in older age groups tend to have higher rates of long-term unemployment. In May 2016, 41% of unemployed people aged 55 to 64 years were long-term unemployed compared with 18% of unemployed people aged 15 to 24 years. (Source: ABS, Labour force survey, cat. no. 6291.0.55.001, Table 14b, Trend)
- Redundancy at age 55 or older often results in full retraining being required to secure work in other industries
- Women are often better equipped to handle retraining due to their experience of this during their working life as a result of pregnancy and motherhood.

If you are in the unfortunate position of being retrenched or made redundant and you are not keen on undergoing total retraining in order to become re-employed, why not consider investing in yourself and reducing your reliance on an employer by doing your own thing? After all, one of the biggest attractions of being in paid employment was the security that a job/career provided – Covid19 has dramatically demonstrated that this security is just an illusion and that the risk of losing your job is very real and through no fault of your own.

Just as technology is creating its own wave(s) of change, as industry after industry are impacted by it and new industries are springing up. Every catalyst of change – Covid19, technology, ageing of our population, as examples in point, brings with it both a downside and an upside.

The downside is the disruption they create and the people that are displaced as a consequence. The upside is the opportunities that are created as a result of the change(s). If we look further at Covid19 the downsides are more than obvious – we are all living through them to one extent or another – so I don't think that I need take up further space on those.

There are upsides though and with those lie opportunities – so let's examine some of those to get you started on being able to think through the downside and come up with the opportunities that will allow you to prosper as a result.

Covid19 Opportunities

There are countless examples of people and business that are thriving as a result of the pandemic. Some have become successful by some clever thinking, others by simply being in the right place at the right time. Here are some cases in point:

Covid19 Support Products

I have a client whose primary business pre-Covid19 and the lockdown was a tourism focused service processing online video stories. Unfortunately, that business was stopped in its tracks with the lockdown, as tourism ground to a halt. However, Grant (the Australian head of operations for the business) had a hobby business on the side importing select spirits and French wines. Through that business he had contacts in Australia that manufactured ethyl alcohol, which just happens to be the main ingredient for hand sanitiser.

Grant quickly recognised that this would become an in demand product going forward and was able to broker some substantial deals as demand for the product soared – creating a revenue stream that would more than carry him through the shutdown. In addition, the people he was brokering the deals with were asking him if he could procure face masks, which he could and did. A second additional (and substantial) revenue stream. There are many other support products and services that fall into this category and I am not going to go through each and every one. The point here is that, no matter what the cause of disruption is, there is always opportunity lurking somewhere nearby.

Food For Thought

One of the hardest hit business sectors in lockdown is the food sector – especially high end restaurants that struggle to transition to a take-away menu. Most have simply shut down and are playing a waiting game. But not Charlie Carrington and his Atlas restaurant concept in Melbourne.

Charlie realised early on that his menu and dining style was not going to transition well to a take-away or Uber-eats offer. He decided to do something different. As his Atlas concept is about the dining and food experience, he asked himself how he could develop a different experience – and he did!

He and his team modified the Atlas menu, so that his customers could have the opportunity to continue to enjoy his culinary creations at home. The Atlas team developed a menu where each dish could be made at home, with ingredients sourced and supplied to them by Atlas.

Except, there's a twist. Atlas dishes are not just a cut up, mix, cook and eat style cuisine. There's a certain amount of skill required, and Charlie bridged that gap by producing YouTube clips that demonstrated how each dish was prepared, cooked and presented.

He promoted this new approach using his Instagram following (it helped that he has 80,000 followers!) but in no time at all word spread through mainstream media. Launched in April, by June they were delivering more meals each week than they used to serve pre-Covid!

Opportunity Out Of Adversity

Jen and Paul Clarke run a promotional products company, "Meeting Innovation", out of Melbourne. The business was started by Jen in 1994 and had carved out a solid niche for itself supplying promotional products to the events and conferencing industry, along with a handful of high profile corporate clients.

With more than 250 well established clients, 2019 was a bumper year and the business generated a little over a million dollars in turnover. Advance orders for 2020 were very strong and, on the basis of that future demand, Jen and Paul placed close to $250,000.00 worth of stock orders in mid November 2019 with their overseas suppliers so that they would have enough stock to service the clients on their books.

Jen explains, "We were really confident that 2020 was going to be our best year ever, based on conversations we had been having with our corporate clients and the events that were booked in for the year, which required promotional products we would be supplying"

She added, "In our business we have to place orders weeks and months ahead of delivery in order to meet supply and shipping timeframes from overseas and these all have to be paid for upfront. We also have to factor in Chinese New Year, when so many of our suppliers shut down for two to three weeks in late January early February."

"January and February are our quiet months, so we did not think anything was unusual when our phones went quiet and incoming emails dropped off – but when things did not pick up in March and then the Government closed our borders we started to get very worried!"

March came and went, during which time every event that the business was supplying to was cancelled or postponed and corporate clients were no longer spending money on marketing.

"It was devastating for us!" said Jen, " not only was our forward business destroyed but the stock we had prepaid for was no longer required, so we were hit at both ends – losing the $250,000.00 we had already paid and having our cash flow wiped out."

"95% of our clients simply haven't come back. Events are not going ahead and our corporate clients are looking for ways to shave promotional budgets. For them, it's about survival and we totally understand that."

Battered but certainly not beaten, Jen and Paul are re-imagining their business, relaunching with a "Covid safe" range of products that will assist businesses to continue to trade in these uncertain times.

"Paul and I thought to ourselves, what can we do? We decided that just closing shop was not the answer. The world is changing and we need to change with it." Jen added.

Jen's mindest is definitely in the Entrepreneurial mould and she is determined that her business will not just lay down and become another victim of the Covid19 pandemic. She explains;

"Government has its part to play but it will not be the catalyst that drags us out of this mess. It will be the Entrepreneurial spirit that will lead by example and give people the confidence to start rebuilding our world – reinventing what we do and how we go about it."

For Jen and Paul energy is everything and, if enthusiasm and a positive mindset are anything to go by, their business going forward may look very different to the business that it was in 2019 but it will be successful.

These are just a few examples of many which demonstrate that, even during a pandemic, there are ways to modify a business so that it not only survives but thrives. There's even a term for this now – "pivoting". You can read of more by going to the support website (www.whencaniretire.com.au).

There are always fresh opportunities to create a new business as a result of changed market conditions and consumer expectations. The fact is that society is always facing change and calamity – some more dramatic than others. Accepting this and recognising the opportunities such events present, will allow you to move forward when others are simply marking time (or, worse still, going backwards).

Many people wonder when the best time to start a new business or side hustle is. You're probably wondering the same thing yourself as you read these words. Well, my answer to you is this - the best time to start is now, today!

The longer you hesitate and delay the less likely you are to actually do something. Yes, you will be nervous, yes, things could go wrong but, armed with a plan, you can achieve just about anything you put your mind to – as long as you are prepared to put in the effort.

If you are one of the fortunate ones who has been affected by Covid19 but will be able to recover reasonably unscathed, you will have the luxury of being able to move forward with a retirement life-style plan at your own pace. However, if you are one of the less fortunate who has been forced into an early retirement or you are facing that prospect, you are going to have to accelerate the process.

In Section Two I will be dealing with both.

For now, though, I think it is time for me to share some of my story – so that you can see that I have already made great strides towards fulfilling the promise of my "longevity bonus".

My Story

Don't panic! I am not about to go into a year by year run through of my life. However, you do need some background on me – how else are you going to be able to put into context the information I am going to be sharing with you on how you can change your life, so as you have more control over what does and does not happen to you?

How else are you going to be able to understand that I am not just assembling a set of theories for you to try out but that I am writing about things I have first-hand experience of?

Like most of us, my formative childhood years laid the foundation for much of my early adult life. At age eight my family emigrated to Australia, settling in Sydney.

For the following six years we moved every year (around Sydney's northern suburbs) until I was fourteen, when we moved to Cessnock in the NSW Hunter Valley. Thankfully I only had to cope with four different schools in all that time, as most of our moves were within travelling distance to the same school!

Then, at sixteen, our family returned to England, where we settled into a town in the North of England called Stockport (where most of my extended family lived). This was a challenging time for me as I was going through my teenage years (and we all know what that is like!) and the culture shock hit me like a Tsunami!

Stockport is where I finished high school, after which I started working in my father's decorating business performing mostly administrative duties. Not long after that we were again on the move, this time to Southampton – via a detour to Portugal.

Southampton is where I got my first job, as a "Trainee Manager" with an electrical wholesaler. Working for my father was not a good idea and I realised that, if I was to become my own person, I had to start to limit his influence over me.

Dad wasn't too impressed with my decision & tried first to convince me that I was making a mistake and, when that didn't have the desired effect, to coerce me into continuing to work for him. He was very insistent that I wouldn't be able to get a job due to my lack of experience.

I took great delight in telling him all about my new employer seven days later! I didn't quite realise how important a lesson this was for me until much later in life and that was – even those closest to you do not always have your best interests at heart and, even if they do, they do not always understand what you are capable of.

Despite my best efforts to settle into English life and even though Southampton was a much better environment than Stockport, as I approached my nineteenth birthday, I came to realise that even though England was my birthplace, it was not my home and so I decided to return to Australia.

I quickly discovered that this was easier said than done. Despite having grown up in Australia, I was a British Citizen (complete with passport) and, try as I might, I could not secure a working visa to return to what I considered to be my homeland – I simply did not meet the required criteria.

After almost six months of rejected applications I was beginning to wonder if I would ever see Australia again on anything but a tourist visa. Then I saw an advertisement in the Southampton Echo (the city's daily paper) calling for people interested in emigrating to Australia to attend a presentation by the Australian Consul at the Town Hall.

"Yes!" I said, "This is what I've been looking for". I went along full of hope, but the presentation focused on everything I already knew – my lack of desired qualifications precluded me from qualifying to emigrate.

After the presentation I approached the Consul's attaché – a rather attractive young lady who came from Melbourne – and told her my story. She took pity on me (although at the time I convinced myself that she was attracted to me – hey, I was nineteen and suffered the same delusions as any male teenager!) and asked me to wait there whilst she went away, returning with the Consul himself!

He sat me down and, over a cup of tea, took the time to hear me out. To this day I don't really know why. At the end of my story he was honest with me and told me that, unless I secured qualifications that the Australian Government was looking for (namely a trade qualification of some sort), I would not be successful in returning to Australia to live and work.

Then he looked at me and smiled and said, "There's more than one way to skin a cat mate" followed by a wink as he reached into his jacket pocket and pulled out his business card. On the back of the card he wrote a name and a telephone number. As he handed me that card he told me to call the number and ask for the man whose name he had written down and that I was to quote his name and let the person know that I was someone who he should talk to. I thanked him profusely and left for home. I was so excited I could hardly sleep!

It turned out that the contact he gave me was the person in charge of a not for profit organisation called the "British Boys' Movement" (BBM). The call I made the next day resulted in me travelling to London the following week to have an interview with him, where I learned that the BBM's charter was to sponsor British boys under the age of twenty one to emigrate to Australia.

They would pay for your airfare to Australia, subsidise your temporary arrival accommodation and even find you suitable employment before assisting you in settling into permanent accommodation.

At the interview I was told that only a small percentage of applicants were accepted and that it could take up to six weeks to be advised as to whether you had been successful or not and anything up to nine months after that before you could expect to travel to Australia.

There were only two conditions involved – one was to pay £20 as your contribution to costs and the other was that you had to remain in Australia for a minimum of two years (or you would have to repay the total amount of your travel & settling in costs).

This was all fine with me as my only other options were to either secure a trade qualification (which would take at least three years) or travel on a tourist visa and simply stay on (illegally). Seven days later, I got my acceptance letter & two months after that I was on my way to Australia.

I was fortunate indeed for things to work out this way, but, in hindsight, I came to understand that I made my own luck – I didn't accept the several rejections I got from the Australian Embassy, I sought out the Town Hall meeting, I did not sit back and accept the information presented at that meeting, I approached the attaché, I told my story to the Consul. I did all of this because I had a vision – a vision I was passionate about and would do whatever it took to make happen.

Another valuable lesson learned – do not let anyone tell you that you can't turn your vision into reality. For the Consul to recognise in me the desire to return to Australia I must have impressed him somehow & it wasn't (I'm sure) because of my charm and good looks (maybe that was a factor with the attractive attaché though)!

He took the time to sit with me, he recommended me to his BBM contact – I also know that he gave a personal recommendation to that contact to seriously consider me. Not only was I accepted into the program, but that acceptance came through within a week (not six) and sixty days later (not nine months) I was on my way back home! Passion, vision, determination and sincerity (some call it authenticity these days) are powerful influencers – never underestimate them.

That was back in 1975 & my life has been a real rollercoaster since then! Mind you, I think that for most people life throws plenty of "Curve balls" at you. It's a well-known saying that it's not about what life throws at you, it's what you do with it that counts. I'm no exception to that.

I have had my share of ups and downs – I have had experiences that have shaken me to my core and experiences that have been pure elation. I have had my heart broken many times, experienced joy and sadness, made decisions that were poor as well as decisions that were good, won and lost battles too numerous to mention. Isn't that the case for you too?

The fact that you are reading this book tells me that you are looking for better ways to live your life – no matter what your present situation may be - and in that respect you and I are very similar. You see, one of my biggest lessons has been to accept that both good and bad thigs are going to happen to us but how we respond to that is what makes us who we are and who we, ultimately, become. I know that I would not be the person I am today, nor would I be where I am, without both those good things and bad happening to me. It is my life experiences that have shaped me and continue to do so. Now, I'm not about to detail all the highs and lows of my life here. However, I am going to share some of these as the book unfolds – especially where they relate to a case in point. For now I do want to share the main drivers of the last eight years of my life as these directly relate to the thrust of this book's themes of being able to adapt to change, so that you can exercise more control over your life than you have probably been used to or thought possible.

Let's cast a backward glance to 2012, because that is where the current chapter of my life really begins – please bear with me as this life chapter is the catalyst for everything that this book contains. I promise that you will find it instructive - to not only set the scene - but to demonstrate that just about anything is possible!

In 2012 my wife, Iris, and I started to discuss what we wanted the next five years of our life to look like. We had just about completed our first five year plan (having got married in 2006). Iris is my second wife – my first marriage had ended in the mid-eighties (yes, a low point for me but some very valuable lessons learned). That first marriage had provided me with two fabulous children (Dennis, my son & Cristal my daughter).

Iris had also been married previously, out of which she had her beautiful daughter, Jasmine, whom I am proud to call my daughter also. In 2012, Jasmine was approaching her senior high school years. We were living in Noosa (Queensland), where Iris was Deputy Principal of a local private school (which Jasmine attended). In two years (2014) Jasmine would be graduating & she had already told us that, at that point, she intended leaving home to move to Brisbane where she planned to go to University.

I provide these details because they were the catalyst for the discussions Iris, and I were having regarding our next five year plan. Iris and I had met in late 2004 and, for all the time I had known her, she had a burning ambition to head up her own school – a career move she had put on hold, as to achieve it would have meant a move away from Noosa, which she did not want to inflict on Jasmine.

When Iris told me that she no longer had that desire for our next five year plan, I was caught by surprise. Instead, she indicated that she would like to explore the possibility of living and working overseas for two years (in Europe somewhere) and how would I feel about that?

Iris is German by birth but came to Australia with her parents and sister when she was only four years old. So, when she told me about her desire to live & work overseas, I could see where we were likely to end up.

To her credit, she was happy to make our destination England, but I assured her that I had no desire to live back in England – loved visiting & really enjoy catching up with my relatives, but it is not my choice of place to live.

We made the decision to explore the potential of living and working in Germany. This became the basis of our next five year plan. Jasmine was to graduate at the end of 2014, so we drew a tentative line in the sand for a move to Germany in 2015.

For Iris, she needed to explore what work opportunities she may have in Germany. Although she is a fluent German speaker, she did not feel that her language skills were at a level that would enable her to teach with the language of instruction in German. This meant she had to source schools that were based in Germany but that taught using English as the language of tuition. For myself, I had to determine what areas of my business could be transferred halfway across the world.

It took us until the early part of 2013 to determine that our "Dream" was possible. Iris had found a thriving international schools community in Germany - in fact it was a global community! All she needed to do was update her resume, source German based International schools & start sending her resume out – she would be applying for teaching positions, rather than leadership positions, as these provided for a more flexible lifestyle. Basically, Iris could enjoy school holiday breaks where we could take advantage of being in Europe and do some exploring of Germany & its neighbouring countries.

At the same time, I had drawn up a plan for my business. At the time, 75% of my income was derived from corporate training, presentations and Executive Coaching, with 25% coming from online activity (I provided digital marketing support to local businesses). I had determined that to attempt to perform the corporate training, presentation and coaching work in Europe would not be feasible. Continuing to service my existing corporate clientele in Australia, whilst being based in Germany, just wasn't going to be economically or logistically viable and trying to establish a similar business in Germany would take at least 18 months – only planning to be there for two years made this option uneconomical.

My plan was to build up the digital side of my business so that I could replace at least some of the income I was going to lose by foregoing my corporate training clients. After more discussion with each other, Iris and I agreed that, although we would take a bit of a financial hit, we could make the move work. After all, this move was not, for us, about the rest of our lives. It was for a two year "adventure" where we could add to our experiences bank without going backwards financially (even though we would not go forward in that space).

So it was that, in the second half of 2013, we started to put more serious effort into planning for a move to Germany. From Iris' investigations into the International School community she had become aware that new hires were generally taken on in the new school year which, for the northern hemisphere, is late August. As a result, we started planning for a move to Germany to arrive in late July 2015. This became very real for us when Iris advised her then current school that she planned to leave in December 2014 (the end of the Australian school year). Before that, however, we needed to tell our respective families. Jasmine was already "In the loop" so to speak, as we had been involving her in the process as we went along. She was very calm about the whole thing because she had her plans for University and a move to Brisbane firmly in her mind and these aligned with our plans.

Iris's sister and brother were both excited for us. Her mother on the other hand was not so enthusiastic. Iris' father had passed away in 2006, so her mother was very focused on her children. Add to that the fact that she and her husband had come to Australia in 1972 for a two year adventure & her reaction to our announcement of a two year adventure to Germany was understandable.

Despite all our best efforts to convince her that two years was our limit, she remained sceptical but did accept that we had every right as adults to follow our own path. This did not prevent her from putting us through a guilt trip at almost every opportunity (especially in terms of "How could you leave Jasmine on her own?").

From August 2013 through to June 2015 we progressively moved our plan along – and there was a lot to organise! We had to prepare our home in Noosa for tenants to occupy for one (we did not want to simply sell up)! So many things to sell, things to store, things to throw out. Financial matters to tidy up, accounts to prepare for international access, insurances to update, policies to revise – the list seemed endless!

I also had an additional detail to attend to – my citizenship. Although I was a permanent resident of Australia, I was not an Australian citizen. I was a British passport holder with a permanent residency visa. However, one of the conditions of that visa was that I cannot be out of the country for longer than two years, or my visa would automatically cancel! The advantage of holding a British passport was that I did not require a visa for Germany – I could live and work there for as long as I wanted! However, I did want to be able to get back into Australia. I decided that the best thing to do was to obtain Australian Citizenship – not a difficult process but a lengthy one.

Let's face it, it was about time! After living in Australia since 1975 I became a fully-fledged "Aussie" in 2014 and by the end of that year had my Australian passport!

Amongst all of that I had the additional task of phasing out my corporate training and presentation clients – some of which I simply terminated, others I passed to colleagues and a few I was able to retain (despite an impending relocation overseas). Whilst, at the same time, building up my digital client base. It wasn't easy saying "No" to opportunities in early 2015 that were going to come to fruition in the second half of the year.

I can tell you now, with a smile on my face, that not everything went according to plan. However, in July 2015, we went to Brisbane airport and caught our flight to Frankfurt, Germany. After almost three years of planning we boarded that plane with both a sigh of relief and more than a little anxiety – after all, this was completely uncharted territory for both of us!

Yes, I had lived and worked in Europe before – but that was in England where I might not have truly understood the culture but did understand the language. Iris understood the culture (at least at a surface level) & was fluent in the language but would working there live up to her expectations and how would I cope without the ability to communicate at the levels I had been used to? These were but a few of the areas of uncertainty we were facing, and all would be answered, plus much, much more over the coming months.

It was with mixed feelings that we arrived in Frankfurt and made our way to our temporary accommodation in Sprendlingen, a town which is nine kilometres south of Frankfurt and which is also home to the school that Iris would start working at in a little over three weeks.

We spent that time familiarising ourselves with the area, as well as house hunting, furniture sourcing and a whole heap of "Little things" that needed to be dealt with. All we had arrived in Germany with were four suitcases – mostly clothing and personal effects with some of my technology for my digital business.

Those weeks were both exhilarating and tiring and here is not the place to detail our experiences – if you are interested in a little more detail on that journey you can catch up on all the details at my blog http://adventuresofadigitalnomad.com/

Suffice to say, we had the most interesting and rewarding time of our lives whilst living and working in Germany. So much so that, instead of the two year adventure that we had planned, we ended up staying for three and a half years – making sure to take advantage of our proximity to so many different cultures and countries.

In addition to exploring much of Germany, we visited so many other countries – Holland, Belgium, Switzerland, Austria, Italy, Spain, Luxemburg, Czech Republic, Hungary, Slovakia, Iceland, Malta, Greece, Egypt, Turkey, Denmark, France and England.

We returned to Australia in December 2018 having achieved all our goals for what turned out to be a three and a half year adventure. Iris got to live her dream of being able to live and work in the country of her birth, reconnect with family and her birth culture. I got to share her joy in achieving that, as well as to prove that the "Digital Nomad" lifestyle is a real possibility and not just a pipe dream. It is that experience that has led me to write this book – so many people we speak to about our experiences are amazed at what we achieved and almost all of them either ask how we did it or state that they could never achieve something similar (even though they desperately want to!).

Here's the reality, anyone who feels trapped in their current lifestyle can escape – if they put their mind to it. I'm not saying it is an easy thing to do, nor will I claim that there aren't risks associated with such a radical lifestyle change but I (and Iris) are living proof that it is possible. Let's face it, Iris gave up a promising leadership career in education to return to teaching on the front line (and in a totally different country).

I gave up a lucrative consulting and presentation business to focus on my digital support services. As a couple we sacrificed a substantial amount of income to be able to make our move.

You know what? We wouldn't change what we did for anything! We have returned to Australia with a different outlook on life and what we want from it. For us, we have decided that our lifestyle is far more important than careers. We now know that we can choose the path our lives take from here on in – the sense of freedom that provides us with is priceless. Those of you who feel "Trapped" in your current situation will understand. Iris and I are now working on our next five year plan and it is different to what we would have imagined five years ago when we were at the precipice of starting our two year adventure.

For you, reading this, I can assure you that no matter how big your dream is, you can achieve it! All it takes is vision, passion and determination, mixed with some planning and focused action. I am hoping that this book will provide you with the foundations of what you are going to need to take your next steps and to be able to do so knowing that what I am going to show you is more than workable.

Enough about me – now it's time to start focusing on you. Let's begin that journey by exploring where your first steps need to be – on examining your mindset and preparing yourself mentally to be able to make the leap from the place you currently are to the place you want to be.

Thinking For Yourself

"Think for yourself, or others will think for you without thinking of you."
Henry David Thoreau

For most of our lives we have been conditioned to follow rules – family rules, society rules, workplace rules. Most of us get used to others making decisions for us but that must change when we become in charge of our own destiny through retirement. An important process in purposeful living is personal management. Personal management is what helps in directing and establishing you on the right path toward your destiny. Personal management is all about the planning, organising, directing, and coordinating various aspects of your life so that you achieve your life's purpose. If you are going to be able to effectively manage yourself, you need to develop the right mindset – an independent mindset that does not look towards others for key decisions.

Personal management is a necessary skill in today's complex world, if we want to realise our full potential. We need to master effective personal management principles, if we're going to maximise the usage of our skills to be able to come up with solutions to our daily challenges. Having the right mindset helps you control your life and build meaningful interpersonal relationships in the pursuit of your passion and purpose. Through personal management, you can break from your confines and live a fulfilled life.

The Four Rules Of Self-Management

If you are to enjoy the sort of retirement you dream of, you must know how to manage your affairs and take control of your life. Unlike the workplace where there is a hierarchy which makes and enforces the "rules" that the organisation bases its processes and systems on (and which the staff then follow), in retirement you are now the person responsible for this. Of course, you are still bound by the rules of society and family, which everyone is subject to, but you now have an enormous level of freedom and autonomy – for most people this is something that they have never previously been exposed to,

With this freedom and autonomy comes a higher level of responsibility – the buck really does stop with you now!

In order to succeed with this personal management and in order to cultivate the right mindset, there are five rules that you need to observe. These rules will act as your personal guidance system as you work toward engaging with and developing your new lifestyle.

Rule One: Work from a "Life map". This allows you to understand yourself - who you are, where you are coming from, and where you are going. A "Life map" provides you with an orientation of purpose and direction. Mapping out your life is the core of every success that you will achieve in your life.

Rule Two: Review your assumptions. Everyone has a belief system and a unique perspective that is used to assess ourselves. Some of the assumptions that you currently hold will hinder your journey to achieving your life goals and purpose. You are no longer active in the workplace, so it is only natural that some of the assumptions you previously based decisions on are going to need to change. Reviewing the assumptions that you hold will allow you to look inside yourself and re-assess your weaknesses and strengths.

Rule Three: Organise yourself and your potential to achieve your desired goals. Without this self-organisation, even the skills that you possess have the potential to be easily dissolved and rendered useless.

Rule Four: Develop your abilities. This includes the development and improvement of your imagination, self-analysis and will-power, along with other skills which may be required for this new life journey.

Rule Five: Take responsibility. Not everything is going to go smoothly – especially as you transition from your working life to your retirement life. Mistakes are going to be made, things will happen to you. However, unlike the workplace, where you could conveniently lay blame for things going wrong on a colleague, your boss or the company systems (and sometimes these were the culprits but sometimes they weren't!), the buck now stops with you! Learn to accept that because it is you and only you that can make changes that will remedy specific situations and improve your life.

Mindset Matters

Your mindset will either be your most significant asset or your greatest liability. The best part of mindset is that it is totally up to you which it is! You need a positive mindset, matched with a strong will, to lead a fulfilled and productive retirement. A positive mindset is not simply being the eternal optimist – that just becomes annoying over time to just about everyone around you. You need the type of mindset that isn't stuck in the rut of winning or losing – it's about learning and keeping trying.

Will refers to the ability to make decisions and choices and act in accordance with them. It is a proactive approach to carrying out the program that you have developed for your life. The extent of your personal integrity measures the degree of will development in your life. The higher the level of your integrity, the more independent your will. Integrity is simply your ability to make commitments and follow through with them.

Effective personal management requires that you prioritise things in your life. In retirement we must become a self-manager. This requires us to have the discipline to organise the various aspects of our lives that are going to contribute to us achieving that "dream" lifestyle we have been looking forward to for the last decade or more.

Your self-discipline of your own value system will keep things in order and will work towards improving and maintaining the quality of your life. This, in turn, will give you the power to do something - even when you don't really want to, if it is in line with your underlying values. This is easier said than done and there will be times when you are not successful at following through with this and that's okay – we are all only human. The important thing is to be able to recognise these situations and times, learn from them and then apply those lessons so that we do not keep making the same mistakes.

This is what experience is – the ability to make mistakes, learn from them and then apply that knowledge in the future. Always remember that it is you who decides what you are going to think in any given situation or moment. Your thoughts and feelings determine your actions and determine the results you get. It all starts with your thoughts – this is why the right mindset is the cornerstone for everything that you do in life.

Smart people take every advantage they can find, and the vast amounts of knowledge available is certainly a considerable advantage. Learn what you need to know to create your new, independent, mindset. This is the fundamental building block for everything else There is simply nothing you cannot do if you set your mind to it!

Critical Thinking

In order to be able to develop and maintain a positive mindset you are also going to need to hone your critical thinking skills. Critical thinking is a key skill that should be applied to all aspects of your life. As a retiree, you need to be able to think critically about the information you are going to need and rely upon for your decision making.

Let's face it, you have never been a retiree before, so there is a lot about this new world that you don't know or understand. As a result, you are going to be seeking out information from a variety of sources – such as; friends who have been retired longer than you, books and magazines (such as this one), professional advisers, etc.

If you are reading this book as a long standing retiree then you obviously are looking for ways to improve your current situation, so the same principle applies. You need to ask the right questions when sourcing and evaluating this information. Before making binding decisions you need to have the ability to weigh up differing opinions and perspectives to help you form your own opinions, to make better quality decisions.

Critical thinking is about questioning and learning with an open mind. It will help you to:

- Interpret evidence, data, arguments, etc. and be able to identify the significance to your circumstances.
- Develop sound and informed-reasoning on which to base decisions
- Use and draw on evidence to justify your decisions and ideas

Figure four is a three-stage model, adapted from LearnHigher (http://www.learnhigher.ac.uk/), which will help you generate questions to understand, analyse, and evaluate something, such as an information source.

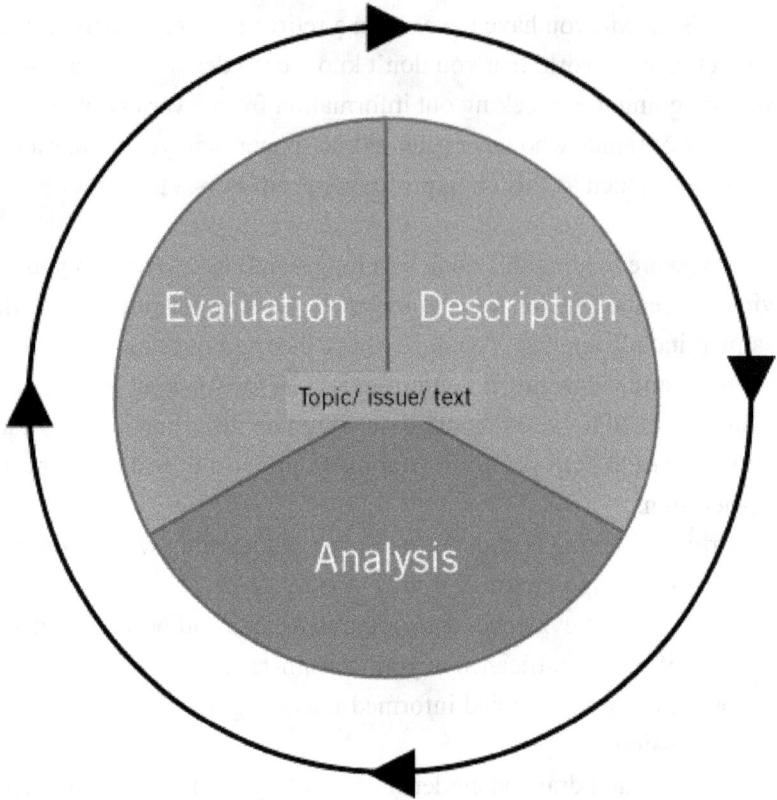

Figure 4: Critical Thinking

1. Description

Starting with the description stage, you ask questions such as: What? Where? Why? and Who? These help you establish the background and context.

For example, if you are reading a journal article, you might ask questions such as:

- Who wrote this?
- What is it about?
- When was it written?
- What is the aim of the article?

If you are thinking through a problem, you might ask:

- What is this problem about?

- Who does it involve or affect?
- When and where is this happening?

These types of questions lead to descriptive answers. Although the ability to describe something is important, to really develop your understanding and critically engage, we need to move beyond these types of questions. This moves you into the analysis stage.

2. Analysis

Here you will ask questions such as: How? Why? and What if? These help you to examine methods and processes, reasons and causes, and the alternative options. For example, if you are reading a journal article, you might ask:

- How was the research conducted?
- Why are the facts/information discussed?
- What are the alternative facts/information?

If you are thinking through a problem, you might ask:

- What are the contributing factors to the problem?
- How might one factor impact another?
- What if one factor is removed or altered?

Asking these questions helps you to break something into parts and consider the relationship between each part, and each part to the whole. This process will help you develop more analytical answers and deeper thinking.

3. Evaluation

Finally, you come to the evaluation stage, where you will ask 'so what?' and 'what next?' questions to make judgments and consider the relevance; implications; significance and value of something.

You may ask questions such as:

- What do I think about this?
- How is this relevant to my situation?
- How does this compare to other research/information I have accessed?

Making such judgments will lead you to reasonable conclusions, solutions, or recommendations. The way we think is complex. This model is not intended to be used in a strictly linear way, or as a prescriptive set of instructions. You may move back and forth between different segments. For example, you may ask, 'what is this about?', and then move straight to, 'is this relevant to me?' The model is intended to encourage a critically questioning approach and can be applied to many situations. When engaging in critical thinking always be aware of **Confirmation bias**. This is the tendency to search for, interpret, favour, and recall information in a way that confirms or strengthens your prior personal beliefs or hypotheses.

For example, imagine that a person holds a belief that left-handed people are more creative than right-handed people. Whenever this person encounters a person that is both left-handed and creative, they place greater importance on this "evidence" that supports what they already believe. This individual might even seek "proof" that further backs up this belief while discounting examples that don't support the idea. Confirmation biases impact how we gather information, but they also influence how we interpret and recall information. For example, people who support or oppose an issue will not only tend to seek information to support it, they will also interpret news stories in a way that upholds their existing ideas. They will also remember details in a way that reinforces these attitudes. No one is immune from confirmation bias, so always run that filter through the information you are evaluating to make sure you can identify where your biases might be and make decisions accordingly. If you are interested in learning more about the way we think I would highly recommend that you grab a copy of "Thinking, Fast and Slow" by Daniel Kahneman – it's a daunting read but very interesting & illuminating!

Defining Success

"Strive not to be a success but rather to be of value"
Albert Einstein

We all crave to be successful – but what does "success" mean? Many of us believe that success brings happiness with it but that is often not the case.

I always remember a quote from the American author, H. Jackson Brown Jr., about the difference between those two terms – "success" and "happiness", it went like this; "Success is getting what you wanted. Happiness is liking what you got."

The late American basketball coach, John Wooden, defined success as follows: "Success is peace of mind, which is a direct result of self-satisfaction in knowing you made the effort to do your best to become the best that you are capable of becoming."

More than anything else, success is an attitude. We all have differing measures against which we measure how successful we are. For some that is money and possessions, for some it is power, for others it is fame – the list is almost endless. Whatever your definition of success is and however you measure it, in retirement you are more than likely going to have to re-evaluate your definition and measurement criteria.

How can you suddenly shift to "happiness" in retirement if you have been unhappy all your life? If you are approaching retirement with the perspective that you will be happy then, chances are you won't be and that could be a huge jolt to your system. You see, the way you think and feel about yourself, including your beliefs and expectations around "success", will determine everything that happens to you.

When you change the quality of your thinking, you change the quality of your life, sometimes instantly. Just as positive words can make someone smile or a well-timed humorous quote can make someone laugh, our thoughts react to the world in real-time. Often, the wider views of society, dictate what the mainstream population thinks that success looks like. Which is one of the reasons that there are so many "successful" people out there who are desperately unhappy. They have passionately pursued the populist "success" dream – they have fame or fortune or power or possessions, but they still feel unfulfilled and, as a result they end up not liking what they got.

I recall a situation several years ago, where I was presenting to a group of would be entrepreneurs at a hotel in Sydney. There were about 300 people in attendance, and I was awaiting my presentation time slot from the back of the room. I had just been fitted with my headset microphone and had about ten minutes before I was to go on stage, to share with those in attendance some key negotiation skills. The presenter that was currently on stage was in the process of wrapping up his presentation when he asked the audience a question - "with a show of hands, which of you in the room considers themselves to be successful?"

There were a few murmurings in the crowd as hands started to be raised. I would estimate that about a third of the room held up their hands. The presenter continued, "so, the majority of you in this room do not consider yourself successful?" (it was a rhetorical question). Then he selected a woman in the front row of the audience who had not put up her hand.

He proceeded to have a brief conversation with her that went something like this;

"Hi, I noticed that you did not put up your hand. Can I ask your name?"

"Michelle" she responded (not her name but it will suffice for this example)

"So, Michelle" he continued, "Why did you not put up your hand?"

"Well, I don't own my own home and I'm not happy in my job, so I can't call myself a success just yet."

"Okay" said the presenter "Let me ask you, do you have any children?"

"Yes, two – both teenagers!"

The presenter smiled and said, "That's fantastic! I'll bet raising two children is expensive and exhausting – am I right?"

"Oh definitely" was Michelle's response. Then the presenter asked a question that shifted the whole conversation;

"Let me put a proposition to you Michelle. If I offered you one million dollars for each of your children, would you accept that? I mean you have invested a lot of your time and money into raising them, so it's only fair that you be compensated for handing them over to me."

"Oh, I couldn't do that, they're my children! And it would be illegal anyhow!"

The presenter responded, "Let's pretend that it's not illegal. In principle, would you sell your children for one million dollars each?"

"No way. I love them. What sort of a Mother would I be if I sold my kids – even if it was for a couple of million dollars!"

Then the presenter thanked Michelle and turned his attention back to the audience and said, "Let's reflect on what just happened here. Michelle did not put her hand up when I asked who in the room considers themselves a success. She does not see herself as a success because she isn't happy in her current job and doesn't own her own home and yet she turned down two million dollars – enough to buy a substantial home and quit her job – because, as a mother, she could not sell her children."

He then paused a moment before he asked the audience, "Who here thinks that working in a job you hate in order to put food on the table and bringing up two children to become functioning, valuable contributors to our future society is the mark of a successful person?"

Here is where things got interesting, every single person in that room not only put their hand up but they rose from their seats to give Michelle a standing ovation. It was one of the most moving experiences I have seen in what was a business event.

The presenter wrapped it all up beautifully by saying, "Success can be many things, just because you are still on a journey doesn't mean you are not successful. Everyone in this room is a success by any number of measures and for those of you that did not put up your hand when I asked that initial question, I would urge you to redefine what success looks like for you."

Five minutes later he had finished, and I was being introduced to the audience to do my presentation. I can tell you; he was one tough act to follow! That is my challenge to you now – to redefine what success actually is for you because without a serious run at that you are likely to end up not liking what you got and, let's face it, at our ages we do not have as much time as we used to for "do overs"!

Retirement is not about rehearsals. This is the phase of our lives where we finally get to make decisions for ourselves that are not driven by the responsibilities we had during our working lives. Retirement is where you can finally transition from the pressures of extrinsic "success" to the rewards of intrinsic "significance". What sort of life do you want to live during your longevity bonus?

If you are not happy – why not? If you do not feel fulfilled, what would you need to do to change that? None of us will ever be remembered for what we got but we will be remembered for what we gave. You should not fall into the trap of defining success through the lens of other people and by that, I mean, that you should be the one defining what success means to you. For example;

A lot of people measure success in monetary terms - the more money they make or have, the more successful they believe themselves to be. However, whilst money is a nice thing to have, it does not really define success. There are many, many people who attain financial wealth that are unhappy with their lives.

Then there are those who take on a definition of success dictated by their family – trying to reach academic and sporting goals, getting the "right" job, marrying a "suitable" person. Often, in wanting the best for us, our families unwittingly put pressure on us, and we can easily end up with a life that our family believes we should be happy with but which, in fact, leads us to feeling trapped and unfulfilled. Society also plays its part in forcing upon us definitions of success – through such things as advertising, media, movies – social media can be an extremely harmful element in this regard with streams of seemingly endless people all having a blast and enjoying success.

Real life is very different though and it is this disconnect that causes a lot of people to suffer from anxiety and depression as a result of not being able to measure up against such impossible standards. However, seeking the approval of others should not be a motivator in driving your definition of success. Sure, it is nice to be acknowledged for your accomplishments, but to actively seek that, and to make it one of your primary drivers, does not lead to success. In fact, having the need for that approval is born out of insecurity and you cannot hope to "feel" successful if that is the case.

In entering your "retirement" years you are entering a new phase in your life and, like any new phase of life, you are going to have to push yourself to accomplish everything it takes for you to achieve whatever you define successful as being. In doing this you will be able to experience what few other people in this world will be able to feel- the ability to enjoy your success in life.

Almost all forms of success bring the pleasure and pride of achievement with them, but few will taste as sweet as success that is self-made and that is defined by you. It is truly an amazing thing to be able to look at your successful life, which includes your passion, your dream, your ability to live the kind of life you want – including your financial security and know that it was you who achieved it! Few people have only themselves to thank for the amazing life they live. This feeling is worth more than any money or material possessions you can think of. It is a feeling that can only be experienced through the success of independent effort.

Not everyone is able to take on the challenge and develop an independent mindset – even though everyone has that potential. The good news is that this book is designed to help you along the way. From mastering the basic skills and personality traits of successful individuals to accessing tools, processes and systems to help you achieve your goals. If you are willing to take on board the information, it will enable you to change your life – no matter where you are right now.

There has never been a better time in world history for individuals to establish their own aspirations and work towards achieving them. The informational world we live in has created a world of amazing opportunities! Success must be defined in your terms! As we advance in years we should, hopefully, begin to establish our own definition of success and have the confidence to aim for that. Only then will you truly be able to enjoy your success because then, you are going to not only get what you want but you will also be happy with what you got!

One of the things that prevents a lot of people from achieving success is believing that their circumstances will not allow them to achieve their dreams and aspirations – we have all been guilty of uttering the "if only…" phrase.

However, it is within everyone's power to rise above their circumstances but, before you can do that, you need to be able to identify when you are playing "victim" and that is what we will be discussing next.

Dealing With The Victim Mentality

"If it's never our fault, we can't take responsibility for it. If we can't take responsibility for it, we'll always be its victim."
Richard Bach

It is all too easy to play the victim and we've all done it; some people make it their life's mantra! When you feel like a victim, you'll end up stuck. Why?

When you play the victim what you are really doing is giving other people power over you. You're basically saying, "oh, there is nothing I can do about this because…. (insert whatever reason you've come up with)". Lifelong victims are depressing to be around – they are always negative and constantly complain about everything. It seems they have a problem for every solution. Albert J. Bernstein summed them up perfectly when he referred to them as "Emotional Vampires" in his book of the same name – they really do drain you emotionally!

I am not suggesting that there are not people in this world who are the victims of terrible situations that were totally beyond their control. Nor am I suggesting that we control everything that happens to us. However, no matter what happens to us, we have total control over how we respond to everything in our lives. Today's world is teeming with bad news – it's overwhelming to some and it is easy to fall into the trap of feeling powerless amidst all of this. In a sense, it is like allowing external influences to define success for us.

Yes, bad things happen. Yes, we can find ourselves in less than desirable situations - but at all times we decide how we are going to behave as a result, and it is those decisions that determine whether the event(s) facing us constrains us or acts as a catalyst for positive change. You see, we can choose to simply "react" – which is a state driven more by emotion than by reason. Or, we can choose to "respond" – which is a state driven by considered thinking.

For many years I was a Coach and Facilitator with the Australian Institute of Management in Brisbane – delivering courses on leadership, business management and communication skills.

In this role I interacted with thousands of people, from all walks of life. I often engaged with people that were stuck in a victim mentality – most of the time they were unaware of what they were doing to themselves. Here's an example; I often had people attend my sessions who were extremely unhappy with their job but felt trapped in the job because "they needed the money". Going to work each day was an enormous drain for them. However, when I asked them how long they had held the job for, most would have held the role for three, five, seven years or more!

Now, I fully appreciate that there are times when you simply have to work in jobs you don't like because you simply have to put bread on the table – you have to provide for yourself and/or your family. We have all been there (I know I have!). However, being in a job you hate for more than twelve months is not an "unfortunate circumstance" driven by economic necessities – it's a choice. A choice you have made over time. Being in that same job for two, three, five or more years is simply a case of playing victim – if you don't like the job, make plans to be able to leave and then act!

This is a classic case of the victim mentality. The person develops a negativity bias and will usually find things wrong with their life or feel that they do not deserve the good things in life. Thus, their life goes nowhere. Sometimes, even when you offer them some hope, they can make you feel like you do not understand them, so they will complain more to show you how miserable they are. If you offer a solution, they will give you another problem to that solution to make excuses for why nothing will work out. The more you try to help, the more they will tell you that you, "don't understand".

With some people, they have been playing the victim role for so long that they somehow get some pleasure in seeking sympathy while being in crisis - because they are at least getting some attention! It's not our job to rescue negative people who do not want to save themselves. All we can really do is ensure that their negativity doesn't rub off on us. If we get caught up in trying to make them feel better, we can get caught in the chaotic negativity and end up going down with them. However, it is our job to be able to identify when we, ourselves, are playing the victim and take steps to snap ourselves out of it as quickly as possible!

How do you know whether you are self-sabotaging with a victim mentality that is limiting your ability to live the life you are trying to create for yourself in retirement?

Ten Warning Signs

1. Your internal critic tells you that you don't deserve the good things in life, that you'll be rejected or someone else will succeed instead. You end up sabotaging the things you want in life, so you do not get them.

2. You feel like a victim of circumstance. Bad things always happen to you, so you expect it or give up before you try. It feels inevitable that things will not work out, so why bother putting the effort in?

3. You lack self-confidence and self-belief. You don't believe in yourself, causing you to not follow through on your ideas. You put things off, find excuses, avoid being accountable, find escape routes, or coast along rather than live life.

4. You let others take control over your life. You let others tell you how to live your life since you feel that they know more than you. By following others, you do not take control of your own life. If you put your life in the hands of others, you have no control over your life. You do not take responsibility for your actions and blame others when things go wrong.

5. You let negative self-beliefs sabotage your choices in life. You give up based on your internal critic. You settle for things in life which support how you see yourself, not feeling good enough.

6. You deplete yourself until you need support. You run around trying to please everyone — to the detriment of yourself — until you hit a crisis and need to be rescued. You stop functioning for yourself when you are running on empty. Then, it is everyone else's fault because you carried them and forgot to think about yourself. Then, you can blame them for not meeting your needs when you didn't meet your own needs.

7. You feel bitter and resentful that you're not living the life you desire. You end up meeting the needs of others because you fear being alone. You give to everyone else, but you are not there for yourself. You don't focus on yourself but instead on living everyone else's life, rather than living your own. When your life falls apart, you end up bitter and resentful at life, not feeling in control. You feel good when pleasing everyone else, rather than focusing on yourself. You rely on your happiness coming from others, rather than fulfilling your own self. You can feel like a martyr, but you're not there for yourself.

8. You make excuses for why you give up. You make excuses or justify why things will not work out, sabotaging your chances because you do not want to put yourself out there to go for what you want and risk failure. You end up escaping the fear of rejection, avoiding failure or being judged. You are avoiding your feelings of not being good enough but end up feeling worse, when you give up and never get to where you want in life.

9. You engage in self-destructive coping behaviour. You seek instant relief when you're not feeling good about yourself, so you attempt to feel better by engaging in addictions, affairs, or other self-defeating behaviours. You end up destroying

yourself and ruining your life by running away from these unwanted feelings.

10. You beat yourself up or self-punish.

This self-defeating "victim" mentality tends to sneak up on us. Ninety nine point nine percent of people in this space have got there over time and without realising what has happened to them. Everyone plays the victim from time to time but truly self-aware and responsible individuals realise what is happening and take positive steps to deal with it.

Childhood is where the "Victim" mentality has its roots. In simple terms this is because, as children, we do not control much of our world – our parents and family do this for us. They do this not to control us (hopefully) but to protect us. Nonetheless, without going all deep psychological on you, as we get older and approach adulthood, we can internalise the belief that there is something wrong with us when we felt unlovable or that we can't control things so why bother? However, as adults we often hold onto the internal critic within ourselves and end up acting-out these self-loathing feelings with self-destructive behaviour that works against us.

You may not see this self-critic deep within you because, as a child, we often ran away from our feelings with self-sabotaging behaviours. But as an adult our world has changed – we can now make our own rules (within societal constraints) and we can exercise control over our environment. The reality is, that we are our own worst critic – often allowing our internal saboteur to shoot us in the foot!

Not recognising the signs of having a victim mentality has the potential to prevent you from achieving your ideal life in retirement. If you have been playing this victim for a long time – "it's everyone else's fault", you find excuses, or you blame life for things that go wrong, you need to take steps to change – and fast. At work, it is easy to lay blame with others – colleagues, management, the company. You lack self-responsibility, and this results in you lose control of your life. But in retirement who are you going to "blame" when things don't go according to the "dream"?

If you continue being the victim the only people around to blame are your partner, family and friends. How long will they be prepared to accept blame before they give up on you? When are you going to decide that the common denominator in all aspects of your life is you? Of course, you could continue to play the role of victim ad infinitum – even in retirement – because you could vent your wrath at the government, the local council, business leaders and all those responsible for creating the world in which you live. In there lies the path to bitterness and, without the focus of work to take your mind of these "Injustices", you will not be a happy camper – and it's unlikely that those around you will be very happy either.

Is this the life you want to lead in retirement? Is that the legacy you want to leave, is this how you want to be remembered? I would hope not! What can you do about it?

The first step is to recognise that you are in "victim" mode. The second is to want to change – the fact that you're reading this book is a hopeful sign of that desire! Next you need to accept personal accountability for the problems/issue that you face. This does not mean that you take blame for things beyond your control, rather, you accept the situation for what it is and start to consider what you can and are going to do to either deal with it or make the best of it.

Eight Steps To Deal With Your "Victim" Challenge

Step 1: Identify the situations when your victim mentality surfaces. When do you display some or all of the following traits or behaviours; blaming others when things go wrong, or if you don't achieve a goal or target, expecting that others will feel sorry for you, rejecting the chance to join in activities with others, refusing to admit that you're enjoying yourself, implying that other people have an easier route to success attracting a disproportionate amount of drama and misfortune, compared with others.

Step 2: Set clear goals and boundaries for yourself. Establish standards of behaviour and performance that you expect. Commit these to writing. If possible, involve your partner or a close friend in this and ask them to point out to you when you do not achieve these. For example, set clear deadlines for tasks and projects, agree checkpoints to review progress.

Step 3:   Create a journal. Record your experiences and results from decisions you make. Reviewing this will reveal your progress without the distortion of selective memory. Journaling is a highly effective diagnostic tool. You can learn more about it in the resources section of the support website (www.whencaniretire.com.au)

Step 4:   Expect mistakes. Not every decision you make is going to work out. When this occurs, treat it as a valuable lesson not as a fatal error. Here's where your journal comes in handy because you can see the totality of your results rather than focusing on isolated instances (of where you got something wrong).

Step 5:   Take on board criticism. The perspectives of the people around you are important too. Make sure that you listen to those people who matter to you. If you have engaged the services of advisors (financial or otherwise) listen to them – why continue to pay for their input if you do not listen to what they have to say?

Step 6:   Establish clear expectations. There will be some things in your retirement that you will action yourself but the majority of your decisions are going to impact on others so you will need to communicate your expectations to those people – both in terms of these impacts and in terms of your expectation as to their level of involvement.

Step 7:   Encourage personal accountability. As well as the need for you to take personal accountability for the outcomes of your choices, you should expect the same from those around you – in relation to their contribution to outcomes.

Step 8:   Maintain standards. Do not allow minor transgressions to set the new benchmark. The boundaries, goals and expectations you established in step two should always be upheld.

Your ability to be able to snap yourself out of this "victim" mentality is crucial if you are to be successful in achieving the sort of lifestyle you wish to enjoy in retirement. If you have been guilty of this every now and then, then your task will be relatively straightforward and, with a few minor tweaks, you should be able to deal with this new level of truly independent self-rule (because that is what retirement is).

However, if you have been playing the victim card for any lengthy period of time you are going to have a hard journey ahead – and it will be a journey that is dotted with setbacks as your "victim" mindset will not go away without a fight! Remember, people with a victim mentality believe that all their ills and misfortunes can be blamed on someone or something else. Their endless dramas and excuses can be damaging for both relationships and success and need to be dealt with swiftly and effectively.

In order to give yourself the best possible chance of escaping this "victim" mentality vortex you are going to need something which motivates and excites you – something to look forward to at the end of all the required mental effort. This is where being passionate about your desired retirement lifestyle is paramount, for it is this passion that will provide you with the motivation to power on through any hardship to get to where you truly want to be. That is what we will be covering next.

What's Your Passion?

"Passion is energy. Feel the power that comes from focusing on what excites you."
Oprah Winfrey

For most of us Baby Boomers, and quite a few Gen Xers, we have been in the workforce for the greater part of our time on the planet. A fortunate few enjoy, indeed love, what they do for a living – but that is not to say that we would not prefer to be doing something else. I was certainly in that category up to 2015. However, for most people in the workforce, their job is what they do because they have to – it's the economic imperative which drives them to drag themselves out of bed each day and go earn a living. For these people, what keeps them going is not their pay-check but their out of work interests – the sports team they play or barrack for, the hobbies they really enjoy, their children's activities, the entertainment they engage with, etc. Work just doesn't excite them and, as a result, it drains them of their energy, their zest for life.

What excites them are those out of work interests. This is where their passion lies and it is often the only thing that tops up their tank so that they can keep going for another week, month, year. This is why, retirement has so much appeal to so many people, "At last!" they say, "now I can do what I love doing" or "I can just sit back and do nothing!"

Alas, doing nothing is not all it's cracked up to be. In fact, it gets very depressing very quickly! And the prospect of doing nothing year after year turns out to be both depressing and frightening in quick time. On the other hand, retirement is about having more control over what you do and when. The question is, what do you want to do and when do you want to do it? Here is where things can get very interesting!

You see, whether you enjoy your work or not, apart from the money, work provides us with structure and, no matter your age, all humans need structure in order to thrive. Work, for all the criticism we throw at it, has given most of us a sense of purpose for most of our lives. It is how many of us (but not all) define ourselves. Let's face it, when you meet someone for the first time, after the introduction one of the first questions we ask is, "what do you do?"

This is why some people fear retirement. They are concerned that as a retiree they will lose their life purpose – they will become less and less relevant to society. We need to stop right there because it most definitely doesn't have to be that way! Your retirement (whenever you are considering making that step) is an opportunity to transition to a phase in your life that should end up being the most enjoyable and productive time of your life. That is only going to happen if you decide to make it so – and, here again, is where your mindset will determine just what retirement ends up being for you. If you think that, in retirement, you are going to have scrimp and save to get by as your health slowly deteriorates and your life comes to an end, then chances are pretty high that this is precisely what will happen.

Alternately, if you think that your retirement will allow you to take back control of your life and do the things you have always dreamed of doing, without having to worry too much about money and still enjoying good health – whilst at the same time still contributing to society around you, then chances are pretty high that this is precisely what will happen. It really is up to you – not the government of the day, the system, the big end of town, those around you – just you.

You are going to need to address two key factors if your retirement is to deliver on your expectations:
- Identify what you are passionate about
- Develop a plan to deliver on your expectations.

We are going to be covering how to develop your plan in section two of this book. Right now, we are going to have a little chat around identifying what you are passionate about. You have to find an answer to the question, "what do I love (doing)?"

Contrary to popular belief, discovering what you love is not as challenging as it may seem. Passion is not a precious commodity that is reserved for a select few -it is a gift that everybody has been blessed with. The only thing we need to do to discover our passion is to have the right attitude. Before we go any further, we need to deal with the elephant in the room, so to speak – and that is, money!

All your working life has been about generating enough money to afford the lifestyle you are comfortable with and ending up with enough money in superannuation and other investments to see you through your retirement.

Well, as I have already covered, when life expectancy was hovering in the low to mid-seventies that was a very achievable outcome. Be that as it may, in a world where life expectancy is now in the low eighties and rising, very few Baby Boomers will have enough to fund themselves for twenty plus years. Gen Xers are in a similar position. You are going to need to address that at some point – and it is better to do it sooner rather than later. Dealing with a money shortfall is always best done long before you run out of it because your options are far more flexible and a whole lot less painful! You are going to need to identify at least a few "Passions" that have the potential to generate revenue – don't worry, I have got that covered. In fact, it is one of the key pillars of this book.

How To Do What You Love And Get Paid For It!

It is said that those fortunate few who do what they love never to have to work a day in their lives – but is that true? Can you truly do something you love and turn it into a paying concern? Does this only apply to a fortunate few & the rest of us are stuck in routines & schedules that we would rather not have to endure? Kevin Hogan, American author and key note speaker, has a lot to say on this subject in his blog (www.kevinhogan.com). I have combined some of his thoughts with my experiences around getting paid for doing what you love...

Imagine being paid a decent amount of money to sit on a beach, engage in some travel, sleep, eat good food. All the time you can stay at the finest hotels, travel first class and pretty much anything similar you can think of...and all you have to do is put in a small amount of effort to let other people in on the secrets of what you learn while you're having fun. Is it possible to do this? How, on God's Earth can you get paid to sit on the beach sipping drinks and getting a tan? Of course, you can! Travel writers & photographers do it all the time – where do you think all those stories about this place or that, come from? A journalist or a photographer gets paid to "share" their experiences in words or pictures. If you can carefully share the experience with several other people, it's no problem. Here's a quick example...

I've been on several cruises. I love them! I even met my wife on a cruise (but that's another story). Mind you, I have always paid for my cruises. I used to work in the Travel Industry in the 1980's & 90's – where I met many people who used to go on cruise after cruise - mostly for free. In fact, many travelled for free and then GOT PAID to take the cruise! It's not a matter of luck & it's certainly not rocket science. So how can YOU do it? It's easy – but it does require some effort & some time to apply some straightforward maths and some scenarios within a defined process. That's what I want to show you, the process that will allow you to identify what it is that you love & how you can get paid for doing it. Before we get into that process, let's look at some ways you can do something that you love & get paid for it. I've picked going on a cruise, but it really can be just about anything.

Option A:

Get 10 other people to go on a cruise with you and you go free – the industry is built around those sorts of incentives. Now, that's not getting paid cash, but you ARE getting paid in the sense of DOING what you love for a week or two with friends/family/colleagues.

Option B: You love cruising and are going to lead a tour of the Pacific with the help of your favourite cruise line. You and your significant other decide you want to go for free. You bring 20 people and take people to some amazing places. You did what you loved with the person you love, and it cost nothing (apart from some of your time in getting people to come onboard, so to speak)!

Option C: You have some expertise in some area. You are pretty good at something. - photography, painting, yoga, hand-crafts, astrology, fitness, bird watching, astrology. You may not even want to travel with anyone, but you do want to travel free and get paid. You simply offer to give some 45-60 minute presentations to interested fellow travellers while cruising. You travel free. And you build a clientele at the same time. Sometimes the cruise company will pay you and let you travel at no cost, depending on how many people they believe will be attracted to your presentations. Any field, any subject. Cruise lines are thrilled to have you on board if you provide "Entertainment" or "Edutainment" and help give other people a cruise they will remember.

That's stage one...

Stage two is all about you building a clientele (mailing list) on the cruise ship by giving your presentations during the trip. i.e. If your offering is convincingly viable you get paid, and you develop a mailing list and you get to vacation in the sun, travel to exotic places and have fun.

Stage three, rinse & repeat – the more cruises you go on (costing you nothing, maybe even getting paid for), the larger your "Clientele" (mailing list) becomes.

"Wait a minute!" I hear you say – "What if I can't think of one of a thousand different ways to get paid on the ship?"

Don't worry! I have that covered for you too:

Option D: You pay for your cruise in full but keep me-
ticulous track of everything you do and how fun it was or wasn't – day
by day, hour by hour. You find out what others cruise passengers do
and do not do on the cruise and in ports - how to get the most out of
that cruise and then you can sell an e-book all about it online. Only if
you are clever…

You opt for:

Option E: Do it right and combine all the above. Total
additional thinking required? ALMOST NONE! Total work required?
Almost none!

Suddenly...you're getting paid well to live the life you want to live.
None of this requires a lot of creativity. That's great – but what if you
don't like cruising or giving presentations to groups of strangers? No
problem!

You can still travel the world, be paid to lay on the beach, eat drink
& be merry. Pick a destination – a country, city, region – whatever!

You make sure that you get 1,000 people to find out how cool your
trip (to wherever you chose) was – Google can help you find the 1,000
people. You put together the lists and secrets of all the places to go &
things to see whilst there. You include the places NOT to go. You put
together the serious info on the things that are a disaster. You make
sure you make recommendations on what food not to eat, where to
NOT to stay, etc. and sell it for $4 online. Now you get paid $4,000 to
go just about anywhere.

Earning money doing what you enjoy is easy. When you like what
you're doing, (and thus probably pretty good at it) a lot of brain power
is not required.

Yet, the experience can't be about you (unless you're a mega star
that people are just dying to find out more on) - if it's all about you,
people aren't going to interested in the least. In order to do what you
love; you MUST be useful to others who would like to do the same
thing or something similar. What if you are not a people person? I
know how you feel - there's a lot of days I'm not, either!

However, there is still hope for you (and me on my off days!) You could consider writing a series of articles for one of the thousands of travel magazines or the local newspaper or some other country's local newspaper. Doing what you love can almost certainly make you money - and allow you to do all the stuff you love for free.

Not a traveller? Don't sweat it – apply the same principles to other activities, hobbies, interests. Remember you are looking for those that **you** like. Just in case your creative mental juices haven't flowed yet, let's go somewhere very basic... What if you love watching TV?

There's a lot of people that make a lot of money reviewing TV shows for online blogs and magazines like Entertainment Weekly, People, etc. Mind you, it's a little tougher making a living watching TV – mainly because it's a lot easier for other people to be just as good as you are at the experience! Nevertheless, people are getting paid to help other people determine what they are going to watch – how many articles or reviews have you read on TV shows & movies? Those articles didn't just happen, they had to be written & that person had to get paid! Why not talk with them?

Here's the simple reality:

Most weeks these people get interviewed by all manner of publications - The Financial Times, Forbes, Cosmopolitan, Woman's World, an international podcast, a local podcast, anyone or SOMEONE who is getting paid $500-$1000 to write an article for their magazine, using that interview as the source of their information. Why can't you be on ONE side of that interview?! Surely you can do something as simple as another human who is earning an extra $30,000 - $60,000 per year. I'll let you in on a secret - often the tiniest modifications and framing of your projects will yield the biggest results.

Case in point – cookery books; have you stopped to think for just one moment as to why there are so many of these damned things? I mean, how many ways are there to cook a meal?

Quite a few, as it turns out - and people are prepared to pay (and pay) for each different way that it is written about. Cooking food has been around for millennia but each time someone presents us with a new variation on a theme people queue up to buy it. Just because there is already a stack of information out there on cooking hasn't prevented publisher after publisher, author after author, from coming up with a new "Twist" on the same story.

Here's another example; you might raise flowers in your garden. You'll get paid nothing (unless you have enough flowers to sell of course) but you WILL enjoy your garden. Good for you, that's awesome!

What if you TEACH people how to raise flowers in their garden? That's a VERY TINY modification to a hobby that could be a lot of fun and brings in $10,000 - $30,000 per year.

Okay. Enough of these simple ideas where you see a LITTLE money following behind you as you move forward. Let's take this a step further. What if you want to make more than a few thousand dollars (or Euros or Pounds) each month doing what you love? Imagine that you love real estate. You get all excited just looking at houses, for example (people do!). So what?

There's a process that is required to have fun, to do what you love and then of course to make a hobby into a SERIOUSLY FUN and PROFITABLE business. "But there are so many people who are real estate investors..." I hear you say. There are! But there are more people who eat (& buy cookbooks or write them!) but you want to do this because it's important to you. This isn't complicated - If it sounds too simple it's because It is.

All you need focus on at this stage is to just change ONE thing about what YOU will do differently in CONTRAST to what everyone else is doing – in whatever field you have decided you want to engage with (in this example real estate).

Then, because you are changing the service/product/experience you must design the process for doing what you love – this is your "Twist" that makes your offering different, unique, appealing. There are probably a dozen or more processes for every "Idea", but you MUST begin somewhere. Start this way:

Plan with the end in mind...put ideas in reverse to figure out WHAT steps you will be doing in your projects. In other words – start at the end and move backwards to get to the beginning. Here's how that might look:

Thinking about the result you want to achieve with the project ask yourself "What is the last ACTION I would need to take before this project could become a reality?"

Write that down. If your goal is to buy an investment property in Sydney, you'd need to have your offer (the amount you are prepared to pay) on the property accepted. That's the last step. Now, for each NEXT "last step," repeat the question. In the purchase of the investment property for example, the last step was having your offer on the property accepted. The step immediately before that would require you to... have the money.

Keep repeating the question (What's the next last step?): Just before that, you'd need to... get approved for the loan; or you would need to... get to the final phase of the money making process you're using to pay cash.

Whatever the process is, you're figuring it out, and NOW, you will be able to refine a process like that to a procedure that can be replicated by anyone that knows how to read (or listen if it's a podcast, or watch if it's a video). That is – other people can follow the process successfully. This is, clearly, a simplified example, but it illustrates the principle. You decide what you want to be doing, and then work backwards to where you are now. And to start with, you only do a very sketchy linear map. Don't fill in the how yet. Just the what.

The key is in developing a process strategy with measurable benchmarks to gauge your progress. You should be able to look at your procedure at EVERY STEP and definitively know whether you are where you need to be or NOT. You need to know the steps to get you to doing what you love so the money follows.

You also need to know the steps to discover precisely what is likely to go wrong at each step along the way so you can prepare for the problems that invariably occur. This is where you need to develop some "What if?" scenarios - to see what could go wrong. You do this for each step/stage of your process.

For each step ask yourself; "What would have had to go wrong for this (step) not to happen successfully?" then repeat that process (for each step) with the question, "What else?", "What else?" until you are certain that all potential "Hiccups" have been identified.

No matter how good you think your process/system is at EVERY step in a process things CAN & WILL go wrong & you need to be prepared for that - so you not only need the success procedure going forward, you need to know what will go wrong while doing the things you love! Then, for each identified potential "Hiccup" develop a solution – a way to deal with the issue in a manner that allows you to continue your journey to that destination (identified as following your last step).

Expect surprises, so be prepared to adapt. And always have measurable progress indicators. They'll help you to keep the faith when things seem slow; or just boring. I have made a pretty big assumption so far – and that is, I have assumed that you already know what it is that you love most. But what if you don't?

For those of you that already know (or think you do) you can skip ahead. Then again, maybe by going through this you might identify something you hadn't really thought of in this context!

What Do You Enjoy Most?

Write down three to five things you really enjoy doing. These are the things you could do all day long, and never get bored. They may currently be hobbies or things you consider to be leisure activities – don't worry about money or income at this point. All we are doing here is identifying what you love doing.

Zig Ziglar told a funny story about this. A guy is watching a football game one Sunday when his wife reminded him that the garage needed painting. The guy moaned to his wife, "I know it, honey, but I'm just so tired. This was one stressful week, and the boss is on my case, and my back hurts. I can't even move myself up off this couch, I'm so worn down!" All those reasons (let's call them that to be polite) are legit in his mind at that moment. Then the phone rings. He picks it up and it's his golfing buddy, Jim. "Bill, I got us a two o'clock tee time. Can you make it?"

Bill jumps off the couch like it bit him, says, "You bet! Just let me grab my clubs! I'll be there before you can walk to the first tee!" and bolts out of the house like a 20 year-old Olympic sprinter. Whilst he enjoyed watching a game on TV he loved his golf – so much so that the opportunity to play completely shifted his mindset from being "exhausted" to full of energy!

What is it that gets you up off the couch when you're stressed out and tired, and gives you the energy you need to get right to it? It's those things you want to write down. Remember, it's not about the money - that's for later. And no, this isn't wishful thinking. If you do what you really enjoy (or are fascinated with), you'll have the energy and make the time to keep going, even when it doesn't look like you're making any progress. Believe me, there will be times when that seems to be the case.

Doing what you love (and getting paid for it) is as much about enjoying the journey as it is in reaching the destination. Once you have your list think about the people you know – both personally (friends, family, acquaintances) & professionally (colleagues, suppliers, customers). Which of those people have some connection to one or more of the things you like to do?

Next comes your skills list. Which of your skills relates (read "assist") to your list of "things that you love" – which are likely to help you make this work?

Inevitably, you are going to come to a point where you say to yourself, "But, my interests are too specialised to make money at this!" Sure, they are! (not).... as if you are the ONE.

Do yourself a favour, get on your computer or smartphone or tablet and head on over to Google and type in just one of your "things I love to do" list items - & press your enter key. Wait a moment for the results & then look immediately above the first search result. You'll see, in italics, a line that reads something like, "About 1.050.000 results (0,76 seconds)". Unless that line is all zeros you are not the only one with that interest – so get a grip and let's keep going!

Most search results will be in the millions or at least hundreds of thousands – don't get bogged down with the number, big or small, it means there is a market and there are pros and cons to both large and small markets. For example:

Small Niche (low numbers) = Big Payoffs

How about mineral samples? I had a client a few years ago who finances his hobby of collecting mineral samples by buying and reselling rough stock - on eBay, of all places! Think about that. He flies all over the world, treks to the mountains to collect minerals (which is his hobby). And then he buys a bunch of rocks from the locals. Then he comes home with these boxes of rocks, sells some of them just as they came out of the ground, and pays for his trip!

eBay finances his vacations, and his vacations finance his investments. That's what happens when you stick to what you enjoy! People will often pay a premium price in a niche market because of its specialised nature - you think you've got a specialised interest? Excellent...you win! The narrower the interest (i.e.; the smaller the niche), the higher the profits, and the easier it is to locate and contact your prospects.

This doesn't just apply to selling information. Those are just examples. Consider... If you really enjoy something, it's easy to enlist the aid of other people who enjoy the same thing.

Case Study

I was presenting at a conference a few years ago and one of the other presenters was this fresh faced 22 year old kid from Cincinnati in the USA. He had become a millionaire through playing video games! I kid you not. Here's the condensed version of what he did.

As a teenager he was obsessed with video games (nothing unusual in that I hear you say!) – he'd spend practically all his waking hours playing one specific game (his favourite). I can't remember the game now, other than it was a multi-player online environment, but it really doesn't matter, he spent so much time on the game that he got to be very good at it – so good, in fact, that he was eventually ranked in the top 3 in the world for that game.

His parents were worried about him – to the extent that his father even tried "blocking" him from playing it, as his school grades were suffering. To cut a long story short, this kid decided that, if so, many people were playing the game, surely some of them would pay him to teach them how to become a "Master" like himself. He was right – and within 12 months he had a series of "E-books" which took people through the process of how to become a game master. Before he left high school, he had earned enough money to not only fund his own university education but had also paid off his parents mortgage!

When I met him, his father was working for him as his business manager – the kid was bright enough to realise that no game's popularity lasts forever, so he looked for the next game that was the "next big thing" and approached the top ranked players to write an e-book on how to play the game to win. He would share the profits with them and, because he was "one of them", was trusted and admired – everyone in the gaming community wanted to be a part of his "system". We live in amazing times!

Back to your list, start to evaluate which of the "things you love" list has the best chance of success for you – remember you want to be paid for doing what you love and the moment that happens it stops being a hobby & becomes a business!

Preparation Steps

You are going to need to have a system by which the business can run efficiently. This means, amongst other things, that you will need answers to the following questions:

What financial resources do I need to accomplish this?

- o How much will it cost? Will I need credit?
- o A consistent level of income?
- o Insurance?
- o Real estate/premises?

What skills will I need to achieve this?

  o What do I need to know how to do?

What contacts will I need to achieve this?

  o Who can help me get there?

  o Who do I know, and who do they know?

  o What do I need to do in return? (Or in advance...)

How much time will this stage take?

  o Overall?

  o Per day/week/month?

What systems will I need to have in place to achieve this?

  o Will I need help, or can I do it alone?

  o What technology is necessary?

  o What will help speed this up?

How can I make this part easier on myself?

  o What can I do to achieve this faster, cheaper, and with less risk?

What else will I need to do, get, or learn in order to complete this step?

Attach your answers to your "step-by-step" sheet and label a folder "project X (name your project)" to keep all the pages together.

Create a timeline for what needs to happen/when - many of the steps will not happen in the same order as the steps they're related to.

For example, if you need a certain level of credit two years from now, or a relationship with a professional, you'll want to start working on that right now.

Once you've done that for each step, go back and look at them again, from the beginning. You'll start to get ideas of how you can do each thing most effectively. And you'll see a pattern forming. You'll very likely have papers all over the place and be jotting notes down that connect a lot of the ideas you've written down. If you're paying attention, the pattern will form around something that feels completely natural, and the ideas will flow easily. You'll be as enthused about the ideas as much as the desired outcome itself.

Look at the whole package you've just put together in the light of the most fun thing on your list, and the biggest goal you have chosen. Do you see how they fit together?

Next, complete an outline of your plan from there. One step at a time, lay out the general steps and timeline. Then fill in the specifics. Now it's time for you to look at your project from the perspective of the "effectiveness expert." Ask yourself, "how can I make this plan simpler?"

Go over every point with that question in mind and get creative. Right now, you're planning and brainstorming at the same time. There are no wrong answers. Just ideas to explore.

Write all your ideas down. All of them. Take as long as you need. Now it's time for a break! Take 10 minutes, an hour, a day (or two) maybe even a week!

On your return you need to look at the ideas you came up with before the breakthrough a critical lens. Ask yourself (for each step/idea):

Will they work?
- If not, can they be made to work?

What could get in the way of them working?
- What can you do to eliminate those elements?

If you just read through this without doing the steps, you are either feeling a little confused, or you are starting to see now it could work and you know you need to actually do this stuff. You do this for each of your "loves" list items - just repeat the process. It gets easier as you go!

Remember, you are not trying to come up with "the next big thing" – you only need a little income to top up what you already have and to reduce your reliance on your "nest egg". Something that is low risk, with a decent Return On Investment (ROI) that you enjoy. It's about creating a lifestyle not creating an empire. That, in a nutshell, is how anyone – yes, even you – can do what they love and get paid for it.

You do not have to be an entrepreneur to do this and you don't need to be a whiz at business – although, once you start making money doing what you love you automatically qualify as being both!

Successful entrepreneurs are simply passionate about what they do, and they make sure that they provide value to their customers. Here are the qualities likely to result in you becoming a successful entrepreneur:

- Self-Motivation. One of the most important traits of entrepreneurs is self-motivation.
- Understand what you offer. As an entrepreneur, you need to know what you offer, and how it fits into the market and provides value to your customers.
- Take calculated risks. We're covering that right now
- Know how to network. You already have many networks you are a part of – clubs (sporting/social), friendship groups, family groups, etc
- Basic money management skills and knowledge. You've been managing your own finances for most of your life
- Flexibility. Being able to adapt to move with the times, avoiding being stuck in a rut
- Passion. We spoke about that only a few pages ago

In other words, you already have all the qualities needed to be a successful entrepreneur! Furthermore, this book provides you with additional insights, processes and tools to enable you to hone those qualities into bankable skills.

The Over Fifty Advantage

This is all very well and good you might say but, surely, I'm too old to be starting something new? Actually no!

According to Pamela Wigglesworth, in her book, "The 50-60 Something Start-up Entrepreneur: How to Quickly Start and Run a Successful Small Business", there is plenty of evidence to show that people over 55 (that's you and me!) are almost twice as likely to build successful businesses than those aged 20 to 34 -even for the tech industry, where younger people are thought to have a head start because they grew up with the internet and 21st century technology. ·

Small business activity rates in the United States in the last 10 years were dominated by people aged 55 to 64 and it is a similar story in both the United Kingdom and Australia. Whilst there is not a lot of research to tell us why, it makes sense when you think about it.

Some factors include:

- A new approach to retirement that technology and modern life makes possible
- Strong professional connections,
- The relative ease with which almost any-one can start a business today when compared to the twentieth century
- Life and business experience (even as a plain old employee!) gained over several decades
- Better understanding of self
- High skill levels
- Measured optimism
- Analytical skills (related to life experience)

Start-ups that survive are more likely to be led by owners over 45 years of age, according to a study, carried out by the Kauffman Ewing Institute, which followed five thousand start-ups from 2004 to 2008. No less than 64% of the surviving start-ups were led by older people.

People over 50 years of age have a greater potential to create innovative companies, products, and solutions. This may surprise you, but the capacity to innovate increases with age and practice. Whether you want to create a start-up in an industry you know well or start afresh pursuing a passion in a new industry, the experience that comes with being over 50 can be a big advantage. The message is simple: being 50 or older is not only NOT an obstacle to becoming a successful business owner (or entrepreneur!) but it also increases your chances of achieving success.

This is a polar opposite to if you are trying to start a new career as a paid employee. Unfortunately, ageism (discrimination based on age) is one of the few remaining areas of discrimination that society seems to accept. Although most employers will tell you different, the reality is that older people are often discounted as viable hires which is why, once you reach 45, that it takes you longer to find a job if you lose the one you have. Why not turn your age to an advantage by harnessing all of that valuable experience and applying it to something you want to do as opposed to doing something you have to do?

A final word before we move on – getting paid for doing what you love isn't difficult, in fact it's pretty simple, but that doesn't mean that hard work isn't required – it is. The beauty, though, of doing what you love, is that it just doesn't seem like work!

You are also going to have a lot of people tell you that you're crazy, that it (your idea) will never work and most of these people will mean well – but don't listen to them! Unfortunately, most people are conditioned to the system where you have to get a "serious" job in order to "make it" in the world. They are so used to trading their freedom (and often happiness) for their income that they sincerely believe that it is the only way. Often, they are too scared to even think that there might be another way.

You don't have to stop what you are currently doing to start on this – get a "side hustle" going. Take baby steps, move from one stage to another & build your new lifestyle knowing that, no matter what, you are going to be doing things that you love (and getting paid for it) rather than sacrificing the things you love because your job doesn't allow you to have the sort of life you really want. If you want things to change – it's down to you. No one will do this for you and a boss (or company) is never going to pay you what you are really worth. Now, what are you going to do about it?

You should also consider how you can build on those "baby steps" to leverage your "side hustle" income and start to create more "passive" income and that is what I am going to discuss next.

Passive Income – Myth V Reality

"Your economic security does not lie in your job; it lies in your power to produce – to think, to learn, to create, to adapt. That's true financial independence. It's not having wealth; it's having the power to produce wealth".
Stephen .R. Covey

The core premise of this book is all about control – providing you with insights, processes and tools to enable you to establish more control over your life so that you can create a lifestyle of your choosing. According to Robert Kiyosaki, author of the best selling Rich Dad Poor Dad, "Financial independence is all about having more choices."

So far, this book has focused on those choices being created on the basis of shifting your mindset from a "living to work" mentality to a "working to live" mentality – with your work efforts centred on doing things that you love and being paid for those efforts. However, when all is said and done, that focus means you are still trading your time for money and, whilst getting paid for doing what you love is extremely satisfying, the money generally stops flowing to you as soon as you stop putting in the required effort.

That is the main drawback of what is referred to as "active" income – where your direct efforts are rewarded with payment and that payment increases or decreases in direct proportion to the effort you invest.

"Passive" income, on the other hand, allows you to leverage your time and money so that you can continue to enjoy a revenue stream even after you reduce the amount of time you spend "work-ing". It sounds great – and if you get it right, it is - but, despite what the "get rich quick" brigade will tell you, making passive income is not easy – that is a myth. It requires hard work, dedication, skills, and a lot of time, amongst other things, to set up a truly passive income lifestyle.

This chapter of the book is not intended to provide you with a roadmap on how to achieve a passive income lifestyle – all I want to do here is point out the option and the opportunity it represents. A step by step program for passive income generation is a whole book on its own!

One such book that I would highly recommend for you to cre-ate your own passive income lifestyle is, "The Five Day Weekend", by author and serial entrepreneur, Nik Halik. In that book, Nik identi-fies an active/passive income generation scale. At the top of that scale are royalties and overrides, which are the kings of passive income.

These include;

Copyright royalties – authors, song writers, software developers and the like continue to get paid for as long as their original works are being consumed. This can go on for decades and the copyright holder does nothing after creating the work but sit back and count the money

Override payments – sales people and mortgage brokers are exam-ples where they continue to be paid a recurring commission for as long as the customer continues to use/purchase the products/services of the supplying company

Share dividends – once the shares are purchased, the owner re-ceives a dividend for as long as the company is profitable and the shareholder retains ownership of the shares. Interest on your superan-nuation savings is another example in this category.

Next on Nik's scale is owning a business that you do not manage – in other words, you employ others to do the work. Your presence is required infrequently, usually for periodic meetings, where your team reports on the status of the business. Franchising or licensing business models are examples of this.

Lower down the scale, as we move towards more active income types, are subscription or membership related services - where people pay a periodic subscription fee to obtain support for their use of the product or service and to receive updates. Software support is a typical example of this.

Then there is owning a business that you work in and manage. As owner, profits from the business are yours but you do need to work on and in the business. This type of income is what we have, up to this point, been focused upon.

At the bottom of the scale (the most "active" type of income) is employment. You get paid a wage each week for performing specific functions related to the amount of time you are engaged in performing the required duties.

Passive Income Ideas

Here are some thought starters for you to consider if you are looking to establish a more passive income stream:

- Create an eBook and sell it online
- Create a training course and sell it online
- Invest in property and earn rental income
- If you have a spare room or two list it on AirBnB
- Buy an existing business and get others to operate it for you
- Create an App
- Design T-Shirts and sell them on etsy.com

The above list is by no means comprehensive but it at least gives you a few ideas to begin with!

Establishing a truly passive income lifestyle takes time – unless you are fortunate enough to inherit a substantial sum of money or win Lotto! However, the principles of mapping out a roadmap to achieve this are all contained in the pages of this book – the planning processes, situation analysis, goal setting and strategy development mechanisms that are detailed in this book will set you up very well to be able to take that next step of leveraging your time and money to be able to create a substantial passive income.

There is an old Chinese proverb which states that the best time to plant a tree was twenty years ago and the second best time is now (today)! The same is true for starting your journey to create a passive income lifestyle – if you choose to go down that path.

And it is a choice. You do not have to create a passive income if you are happy to work at something you love and be paid for it – but it is nice to know that the option exists and is achievable, if you choose to go down that path.

Whether you elect for a more active income lifestyle or passive there are going to be risks that are associated with both. Let's have a look at risk taking next.

The Risk Factor

"Security is mostly a superstition. Life is either a daring adventure or nothing."
Helen Keller

Playing it safe is the default option for most of us but in playing it safe, we often lull ourselves into a false sense of security. When was the last time you took a risk – a real nail biting, sit on the edge of your seat, almost scared to death risk? This doesn't have to be a life threatening, physical risk. It can be anything that makes you feel nervous – something that really takes you out of your comfort zone. The bottom line with risk is that it is all around us – you can't eliminate risk from your life – all you can do is manage it and to be able to do that you need to have a handle on two things:

1. What your tolerance toward risk is
2. Identifying the risks, you are likely to face

Before we go into all of that. Let's start with a definition of what we are talking about when we mention that word, "risk". Risk is present in all walks of life – in business, our personal lives and most definitely in retirement.

In business the term "risk" refers to a threat to the company's operations or ability to achieve its financial goals. A business risk means that a company's or an organisation's plans may not turn out as originally envisioned or that it may not meet its targets. Such risks cannot always be blamed on the stakeholders of the company, as risk can be influenced by various external factors such as; rising prices of raw materials, increased competition, changes and additions to existing regulations set by the government – such as those we are currently experiencing as a result of the Covid19 pandemic, etc. In our personal lives "risk" is classified as anything that exposes you to the risk of losing something of value. Financial investments are a good example but there are many more, including; your health status, making poor decisions, involvement in accidents, etc. At its core, risk is the potential for uncontrolled or unexpected loss of something of value. Whenever we take a "risk" we are entering into an intentional interaction with uncertainty. Uncertainty is a potential, unpredictable, and often uncontrollable outcome - risk is an aspect of action taken in spite of uncertainty.

Risk Identification

When it comes to retirement, we are definitely entering into uncharted territory for ourselves – after all, we haven't been retired before, so we are not sure what, precisely, is going to happen. What matters most with our exposure to risk is our reaction – because that will be a big factor in determining the impact the risk is likely to have on our lives. Our reaction can be anything from feeling slightly anxious about the situation, through to worry, anxiety all the way to terror.

Our responses to risk (or any type of danger) are hardwired into our brains and linked to our survival instincts. It's a complex topic and one that is way outside the scope of this book. However, you are going to need to at least have a basic understanding of what happens to us when we face risks and, importantly, how you can become a better manager of the whole process.

Our preferred state of being is our "Comfort zone", that place where things feel familiar to a us and we are at ease and in control of our environment. It is here that we experience low levels of anxiety and stress - in this zone, a steady level of performance is possible.

This is not the space in which we perform at our best. Peak performance only happens when we stretch ourselves - sometimes you have to step out of your comfort zone and challenge yourself. The irony with the comfort zone is that staying in that zone for too long will make you complacent – we get bored and become lazy.

The graph in Figure five illustrates this.

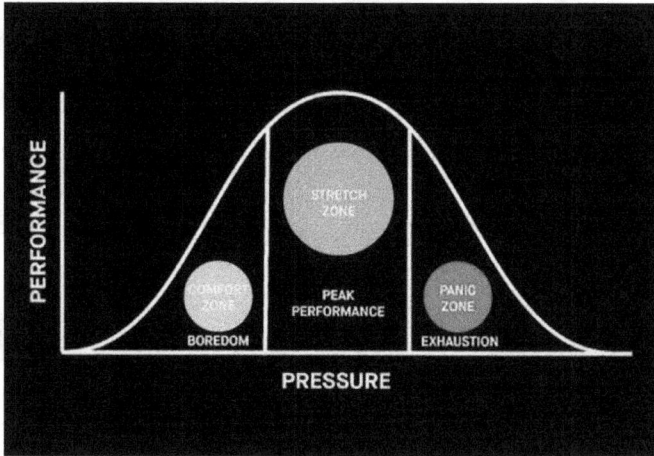

Figure 5

In the workplace, our natural tendency to want to stay in the comfort zone is balanced by our employer (if you work for an organisation
or person) or our customer (if you are in business for yourself) forcing
us to step out of the zone by making additional demands of us or in-
sisting we do things differently, often resulting in further training or
upskilling of some sort.

We, ourselves, also contribute to this zone movement whenever we
take on added responsibilities (for an increase in pay or better conditions) or start a new job. In early retirement, the absence of those
forces isn't generally an issue because you are in a situation where,
although you have (hopefully) planned for it, there are so many new
things to deal with that you automatically default to the growth/peak
performance zone. What happens as you get used to your new environment? Unless you can regulate yourself (which is difficult) your
tendency to want to stay where you feel comfortable is going to work
against you in the long run. Stepping out of your comfort zone isn't always easy but it is necessary – even when you are retired.

For all that, though, there are a couple of provisos:

1. You do not want to be out of your comfort zone all the time. It's too exhausting and, ultimately, will lead to high levels of stress – which is both unhealthy and leads to poor performance (ref Fig 4). The trick is to get into the growth zone for short bursts and allow yourself to ease back into the comfort zone where you can relax and recharge a little before your next burst.

2. You should not put yourself in a situation that absolutely terrifies you. Being scared is one thing, you can move through it, but terror is another thing entirely – it results in paralysis and overwhelm where you will simply freeze and not do anything or run as fast as you can away from the source.

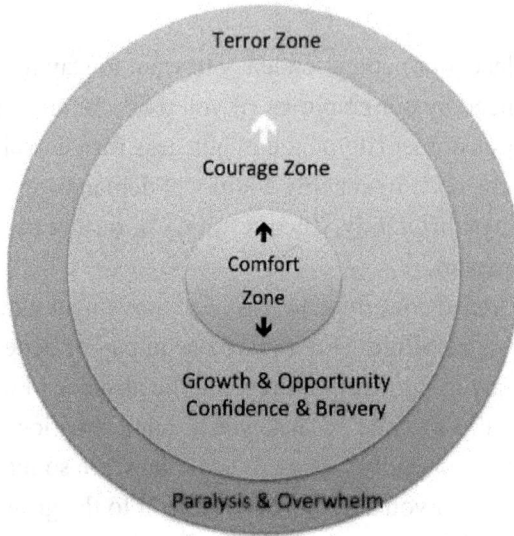

Terror Zone

Courage Zone

Comfort Zone

Growth & Opportunity
Confidence & Bravery

Paralysis & Overwhelm

Figure 6

Figure six illustrates this principle well.

If you are going to be able to self-regulate the movement between your comfort zone and your discomfort/growth zone whilst, at the same time, avoiding the terror zone, you will need to be able to both identify risks and develop strategies to deal with them. This Is what "Risk Management" is all about.

Risk Management is the process of identifying, analysing and responding to the risk factors that you are likely to face throughout your retirement. This allows you to exercise far more control over your future, leading you to be proactive rather than reactive.

For example: The current life expectancy for Australian men is eighty years. If you retired at sixty seven you are likely to have at least thirteen years of retirement. There is a risk here that your financial reserves may not last that long – let's face it, thirteen years is a long time and almost anything could happen during that time that could impact on your finances.

A reactive person with high risk tolerances may not be concerned about this for their first five years of retirement because their finances look good at sixty seven – but by seventy two that nest egg is looking decidedly different and now the worry starts to set in. The person waited five years to identify the risk they now have limited options to deal with it.

On the other hand, a proactive person with a lower risk tolerance identified this risk at the outset and developed strategies to deal with it – in the event it became an issue. Instead of being worried, this person simply acts as per their risk management plan and the outcome is vastly different. Proper risk management will reduce not only the likelihood of an event occurring, but also the magnitude of its impact. Here's what you need to know in order to develop your own risk management strategies leading up to and during retirement.

Risk Management Systems

Risk Management Systems are designed to do more than just identify the risk. The system must also be able to quantify the risk and predict the impact of the risk on the matter at hand. The outcome is a risk that is either acceptable or unacceptable. The acceptance or non-acceptance of a risk is usually dependent on your tolerance level for risk.

Risk management needs to be a continuous process. If risk management is set up as a continuous, disciplined process of issue identification and resolution, it starts to become second nature to you. Surprises will be diminished because emphasis will now be on proactive rather than reactive management. You need to establish this process early on and identify all of the possible risks that might impact on your retirement plans -you must choose those which are the most likely to occur. That assessment would be based largely upon past experience regarding the likelihood of occurrence, gut feel, lessons learned, historical data (such as the experience of others), etc. You may also need to have conversations with trusted advisors (such as an accountant or investment adviser).

The risks you are going to face as you approach your retirement are going to be very different from other people (although there will be some common risks). This is because your circumstances will be unique for you and your view on what constitutes a risk will differ from other people (one person's risk is another person's normal).

To give you a bit of a kick start in this space here's a few areas that risks can found in:

- Social - friends and family.
  - What if one of your children asks to move back home for a while – how would that impact you?
  - A good friend falls on hard times and asks for some financial support. How do you deal with that?
- Environmental
  - A new road is going to be built and your home is going to be compulsorily purchased. Now what?
  - A new shopping centre is going to open, turning your quiet street into a major thoroughfare. Your response?
- Inflation
  - Increases from 3% per annum to 8% per annum. What will that do to your spending power over the following five years?

- Government
  - Tax on superannuation is raised by 10%. What does that mean for you?
  - The family home is no longer exempt from your net worth assets calculations. How will this impact you?

I'm sure you get the picture! Risks can arise out of nowhere and from just about anywhere – again Covid19 is a classic example of an unexpected event increasing your exposure to risk. You need to be aware of what your risks are and could be. When my wife and I were planning our two year "Adventure" to Germany, we identified a number of risk (or "what if?") scenarios. Rather than allow these to prevent us from moving forward, we instead developed a risk management strategy which allowed us to engage our plan with more confidence.

These included;

- What if it takes us longer than four weeks to find permanent accommodation?
- What if my wife cannot find suitable employment?
- What if a member of our family in Australia becomes seriously ill whilst we are away?
- What if my wife cannot secure an appropriate working visa in Europe?
- What if either of us hates Germany?

Those were just a few of the risks we identified and for each we had to evaluate how serious it would be for us if they eventuated and what we would do if that happened. Despite all of our planning we experienced setbacks we did not plan for, risks we just didn't think about – and that will happen to you too. That's life! However, what we did find is that the risk management process we had followed in planning for the move provided us with a framework to better deal with those unexpected situations that arose. We simply applied that process to the (up until then) unforeseen event and dealt with it. Having identified the risks you are likely to face you then need to consider risk responses. This generally includes one of four core strategies:

1. Avoidance (eliminating a specific threat, usually by eliminating the cause)
2. Reduction (reducing the expected impact of a risk event by reducing the probability of occurrence)
3. Sharing (transfer – outsource) – insurance is a great example of this.
4. Retention (accepting the consequences of the risk)

In developing contingency plans, you engage in a problem solving process. The end result will be a plan that can be put in place on a moment's notice – should the risk eventuate. What you want to achieve is the ability to deal with blockages and barriers which represent a risk to your retirement plans. Having contingencies in place ensures that you can quickly deal with most problems as they arise. This approach provides a rational basis for better decision making, in regard to all risks, rather than knee jerk emotional reactions. If you don't actively attack risks, they will actively attack you!

Risk Analysis

Having identified your risks, next you need to analyse them. The risk analysis process is essentially a problem solving process.

Select the identified risk

• Categorize and prioritise the risk.

It is likely that you will have a long list of risks Prioritising will assist you to manage those risks that have both a high impact and a high probability of occurrence.

You can access a tool to help you with this at the support website (www.whencaniretire.com.au). Below is an illustration of the matrix that this tool will help you complete.

RISK ASSESSMENT MATRIX

Likelihood	Insignificant (A)	Marginal (B)	Moderate (C)	Critical (D)	Catastrophic (E)
Unlikely (1)	Low risk. No further action	Low risk. No further action	Low risk. No further action	Low risk. No further action	Medium risk. Further action optional
Seldom (2)	Low risk. No further action	Low risk. No further action	Medium risk. Further action optional	Medium risk. Further action optional	High risk. Further action necessary
Occasional (3)	Low risk. No further action	Medium risk. Further action optional	Medium risk. Further action optional	High risk. Further action necessary	Extreme risk. Act now
Likely (4)	Medium risk. Further action optional	Medium risk. Further action optional	High risk. Further action necessary	Extreme risk. Act now	Extreme risk. Act now
Definite (5)	Medium risk. Further action optional	High risk. Further action necessary	Extreme risk. Act now	Extreme risk. Act now	Extreme risk. Act now

Consequence

Figure 7

The matrix in Figure seven places your identified risks into one of four categories

- o Low risk – No action required
- o Medium risk – Further action optional (depending on your risk tolerance profile)
- o High risk – Further action necessary
- o Extreme risk – Act now!

This is achieved by rating each risk in terms of likelihood (vertical axis) and consequence/impact (horizontal axis)

- • Assess the Risk.

Traditional problem solving often moves from problem identification to problem solution. However, before trying to determine how best to manage risks you should try to identify its root cause.

Ask yourself questions such as:

- o What would cause this risk?

- How will this risk impact my retirement?

Develop Responses to the Risk

Now you are ready to begin the process of assessing possible remedies to manage the risk or possibly, prevent the risk from occurring.

Questions you ask yourself at this stage include:

o What can be done to reduce the likelihood of this risk?

o What can be done to manage the risk, should it occur?

- Develop a Contingency Plan or Preventative Measures for the Risk

Here is where you will convert, into tasks, those ideas that were identified to reduce or eliminate risk likelihood. Those tasks identified to manage the risk, should it occur, are developed into short contingency plans that can be put aside. Should the risk occur, they can be brought forward and quickly put into action, thereby reducing the need to manage the risk by crisis and avoiding those emotional knee jerk responses that most people make.

Once risks have been identified and analysed, all techniques to manage the risk fall into one or more of these four previously mentioned major categories:

1. Avoidance (eliminate, withdraw from or not become involved)
2. Reduction (optimise – mitigate)
3. Sharing (transfer – outsource) – insurance is a great example of this.
4. Retention (accept and budget accordingly)

As risk management is an ongoing process you should be monitoring and Reviewing your exposure to risks on an ongoing basis. Be prepared to add/remove risks from your management plan as your circumstances or environment changes. Always remember that no plan, no matter how detailed and well thought out, survives intact once implemented. You are going to face challenges as you start to live your retirement lifestyle.

Your risk management plan and processes will allow you to better manage your circumstances and give you more control of your life.

Remember;

- Risk perceptions are personal – high risk to one person is low to another.
- Timing is also important – some days you have lower risk tolerance than others – depending on your energy levels and mood.
- We all face risks so, regardless of your tolerance towards it, you need to have a process by which you can manage it.
- Do not risk too much of your capital (superannuation/savings) or equity (in property) – it has taken you too long to build up & you no longer have time on your side to rebuild or replenish anything you lose.
- Do not fall into the "start-up trap" where you put in too much time and effort to get your business idea up and running to the detriment of your personal relationships. Yes, you will need to put in some hard yards to get things going but if this is any longer than 12 months, I suggest you go with a different idea. You are wanting to create a lifestyle which rewards your long years of personal and professional sacrifice not embark on another stressful and unrewarding career.

And They Said It Couldn't Be Done

"Never interrupt someone doing what others said couldn't be done."
Amelia Earhart

As you read through this book you are going to come to have more belief in the notion that you can have more control over your life in your later years – for that matter, anyone can have more control in their lives at any time, if they simply shift their thinking and stop blindly accepting the narrative they are told day after day. That being the case though, this book is really focused on those who are approaching retirement or at least starting to give the concept more than just a passing thought. As your belief in your ability to actually do this grows, you are going to start sharing your thoughts with others – and why not? It's exciting when you come to realise that you can free yourself from your present day to day shackles and live the life you choose!

Not everyone you share your epiphany with is going to understand and these people will become your single biggest obstacle (after yourself) to overcome – especially those closest to you, whose opinions you value. Then there are the countless "experts" out there who will tell you, with one hundred percent conviction, that what you are considering is madness. They will point out all of the reasons why your thinking is flawed and why your plan can only ever end in heartbreak. These people will do their best to convince you that your best strategy is to "stick with the program" – you know the one, work hard all of your life then enjoy your retirement.

We've already covered why, in the twenty first century, that thinking is flawed. Unfortunately, for those that listen to this reasoning and decide not to "risk" it, they will not enjoy the freedom that they deserve and, by the time they are forced to accept that retirement is not what had been promised to them, it is too late. Why do we allow ourselves to be manipulated by so called "experts" with their incessant doomsday predictions & outlandish claims as to what will or will not happen in the near future (anything from a few years to a few decades)?

There isn't a week that goes by where some naysayer, somewhere, with credentials to prop up their claims, is quoted in the media, or has a "scientific" report published.

As a Digital Nomad I am very interested in what the future (especially the next decade) has in store for society as, if I can get ahead of - or at least keep up with - the curve, I can leverage that into income. Here are some examples of what I'm talking about:

"The Americans have need of the telephone, but we do not. We have plenty of messenger boys." This statement was made by Sir William Preece, Chief Engineer of the British Post Office in 1876.

"Television won't be able to hold on to any market it captures after the first six months. People will soon get tired of staring at a plywood box every night." Stated Darryl Zanuck of 20th Century Fox in 1946. Had the appearance of the television not progressed, he would probably have been quite correct. In those days the difference between watching a TV at home and going to the cinema was vast, and Zanuck couldn't foresee the advance in screen size and quality of picture on a television set.

"Everyone's always asking me when Apple will come out with a cell phone. My answer is, 'Probably never." I don't think there is any excuse for this most misguided prediction from David Pogue in the New York Times in 2006, as the first iPhone was introduced in 2007.

"Two years from now, spam will be solved." This was an observation by Bill Gates of Microsoft in 2004. He doesn't predict how spam will be stamped out, but he was way off the mark as spam currently accounts for over 90% of all emails sent!

"No-one will need more than 637kb of memory for a PC." Bill Gates (again) in 1981 – although he denies ever saying it – mind you, I think I'd be denying that one!

"There is no reason for any individual to have a computer in his home." Ken Olsen, founder of Digital Equipment Corp, Circa 1958.

"I predict the Internet will soon go spectacularly supernova and in 1996 catastrophically collapse." 1995 Robert Metcalfe, founder of 3Com, inventor of Ethernet, tech pundit and columnist.

"We'll soon buy books and newspapers straight over the Internet? Uh, sure." (as in no way!) Clifford Stoll, astronomer and author 1995.

"There's just not that many videos I want to watch." Steve Chen, CTO and co-founder of YouTube. Chen's concern in 2005 about YouTube's long-term viability was put to rest two years post-launch, when Google paid $1.65 billion to acquire the site.

"We will never make a 32-bit operating system." (Most systems are now 64-bit) Bill Gates, co-founder and chairman of Microsoft 1989

"I think there is a world market for maybe five computers." Thomas Watson, president of IBM, 1943

"Nuclear-powered vacuum cleaners will probably be a reality within ten years." Alex Lewyt, president of Lewyt vacuum company, 1955

With hindsight it's easy to scoff at all of those but, at the time, these people were recognised experts in their respected fields & yet they were oh so wrong! Then there are the academic & scientifically based "Time bombs".

Here's a couple of quick examples:

Claim one:

In 1968, Paul R. Ehrlich wrote "The Population Bomb" and declared that the battle to feed humanity had been lost but going on to claim that there would be a major food shortage in the US. "In the 1970s ... hundreds of millions are going to starve to death," and by the 1980s most of the world's important resources would be depleted. He forecast that 65 million Americans would die of starvation between 1980-1989 and that by 1999, the US population would decline to 22.6 million. Hasn't happened (so far) although this guy is still paraded out by the media as an "expert" in the field every time world population & overcrowding is brought up.

As an aside – with our population at 7 billion, if every person on the planet lived as densely as they do in Manhattan (New York, USA), the whole world could easily live in New Zealand!

Claim Two:

During the 1970s the media promoted global cooling alarmism with dire threats of a new ice age. Extreme weather events were hyped as signs of the coming apocalypse and man-made pollution was blamed as the cause. Environmental extremists called for everything from outlawing the internal combustion engine to communist style population controls. Time magazine even ran a cover story in 1972 Called, "The Big Freeze" Noted scientist Sir Fred Hoyle even wrote a book on the matter – aptly named "Ice".

Claim Three:

In 1989, "using computer models", researchers concluded that global warming would raise average annual temperatures nationwide two degrees by 2010." (Associated Press, May 15, 1989). The actual result: According to NASA, global temperature has increased by about

0.7 degrees Fahrenheit since 1989. And U.S. temperature has increased even less over the same period.

This one is still raging but the bottom line is this – none of the United Nations Intergovernmental Panel on Climate Change (IPCC) predictions has come true in over 30 years of published research & yet, year after year, their report on the so called state of our climate is given traction by a headline hungry media. Strangely enough, that council's operating budget continues to increase & governments, globally, are pushing for all sorts of levies & taxes in the "fight against climate change".

Be very wary of accepting anyone's predictions about the future – especially the so called experts who, in my opinion, are simply giving it their best guess. Let's face it, 99% of those in the finance & banking industry didn't see the GFC coming in 2008 & those that did were (mainly) trying to cover it up anyhow – leaving us all in the dark. Experts are just as capable at getting it wrong as novices – after all, the Ark was built by an amateur (Noah) whist the Titanic was built by experts. Bear that in mind the next time you seek expert advice.

What about those friends and family members who, whilst not predicting the future, are advising you to "stick with the program"? My suggestion is this, for those family members that could be impacted by your decisions going forward - such as your spouse or partner or any dependant (adult) children, I would suggest that you provide them with the information you have at hand that is influencing your current thinking. They should, at least, have access to that. More information on this will be provided in section two.

For the rest, by all means state your case but do not allow them to change your mind. After all, it is not their lives that will be impacted by your decisions here, so they do not really have any "skin" in the game – just because they want to live in the hope that the fantasy retirement story is true (despite all evidence to the contrary) doesn't mean that you have to stay there with them! The future is an uncertain place for us all – wanting to "know" what lies ahead is a natural instinct but believing the guesswork of others or heeding the advice of relatively uninformed friends and family is something that no intelligent, reasoned, person should be doing.

Don't be lazy - if you see a prediction that scares or intrigues you or someone tells you something that challenges your current thinking – research it (thoroughly), undertake a risk analysis on it, apply critical thinking principles (we covered those earlier) and then come to your own conclusions. At least that way you will be able to exert more control over your life – and your future.

One thing about our future that is certain – information is going to continue to be more accessible, so there really is no excuse for accepting anyone else's word at face value. That increased availability of information will add further fuel to the fires of disruption and, if you want to avoid becoming a victim in all of that you will need to have a plan.

Developing your plan is what section two is all about but, before we get to that, let's quickly recap what has been covered in section one.

Section One Summary

We have covered quite a bit of ground in setting the tone for the rest of the book. Here's a quick refresher before you start to read section two.

A WORLD OF ENDLESS POSSIBILITIES

- We live in amazing times, nonetheless, there are challenges we must face as our world continues to change on both a societal and personal level
- Population age demographics are shifting to an older spectrum
- Our current retirement model is outdated
- You need to take back control of your life

YESTERDAY'S THINKING IN TODAY'S WORLD

- Advances in technology are driving changes in business and this is filtering into changes to society as a whole
- Future gazing and predictions are often wrong because of flawed modelling
- Disruption/change brings with it opportunities if you ask the right questions and look in the right places
- Why our thinking around retirement needs to change to embrace the longevity bonus and deal with the age wave
- The Gig economy changes everything

MY STORY

- How vision and determination shape our lives
- We are all the result of our experiences

- 2012 as a watershed year
- 2015 putting the plan into action
- You do not have to remain trapped by your circumstances. We each have the power to exercise choice over what we do and where we are

THINKING FOR YOURSELF

- The four rules of self-management
- Your mindset matters, if you believe you can achieve
- The importance of critical thinking – digging below the surface, asking the right questions

DEFINING SUCCESS

- Success is subjective – it's an attitude
- Success does not mean happiness
- Retirement as an opportunity to redefine success in your own terms

DEALING WITH THE VICTIM MENTALITY

- The importance of taking personal responsibility
- Do not allow your circumstances to trap you
- No matter what happens to us we are always in control of how we react or respond
- Warning signs and the eight steps to deal with the challenges of the victim mentality

WHAT'S YOUR PASSION?

- Passion build energy
- The workplace as an environment providing you with structure
- Determining the structure, you desire for your retirement
- Identifying what you are passionate about and how to use this as a basis for generating additional/supplemental income
- The over 50 advantage

PASSIVE INCOME – MYTH V REALITY

- Leveraging your time and money

- The active-passive income scale
- Choices and options

THE RISK FACTOR

- Life is risk – security is an illusion
- How to identify your risk tolerance profile
- Identifying and classifying your risks
- What is your comfort zone and why you need to break out of it occasionally?

AND THEY SAID IT COULDN'T BE DONE

- Dealing with negativity and naysayers
- There are always reasons why something may not work but that is what risk analysis is for
- Take expert advice with caution – use critical thinking to evaluate

---

Planning Your Journey

So far, I've established that the social/work structure most western cultures are based upon is flawed – basically, the foundations that this structure is built upon no longer exist.

You can probably argue that some, if not all, the conclusions I have come to are flawed (hey, no one is perfect!). However, here is one undeniable fact that you cannot argue – we are going through an unparalleled level of change, both in its scope and pace, and those changes are impacting every corner of society. Some of these changes affect certain sectors of our community more than others. Notwithstanding that, the flow on effects are bound to affect you – and probably sooner than you are thinking. In light of this, it makes sense to reconsider your position on your retirement plans. You should be considering what you are going to do with your longevity bonus.

I'm assuming that if you are reading this you are within ten years of reaching your retirement milestone – for most of us that ten year window is when reality starts to bite and we realise that, left unattended, our plans (or lack thereof) for our later years are not going to cut it for us. Whether you are sitting comfortably in that ten year zone, are facing a forced retirement due to redundancy or you are within touching distance of retirement (say, two or three years away) this section of the book is going to show you how to create your own, personal, roadmap for this latter part of your life. Then again, you may be nowhere near retirement, but you are looking to change your current situation – you simply do not want to continue on your present course.

Any course of action, which carries with it substantial risks, is deserving of your attention. If you are to put yourself in the best possible position to take advantage of the opportunities that your latter years present you, you're going to need to pace yourself and you are going to need to have a plan. I would strongly suggest that you read through this section of the book in its entirety before starting on your plan. Once you have digested those contents and have been introduced to my retirement planning process, you can then start to put your own plan together.

What you do need to be aware of before you start on this section is that there is a lot of information to digest here. Some of it is likely to be familiar to you, so this will be a great reminder and refresh opportunity but some will not and that content is going to require you to be able to focus on the concepts and ideas detailed, in order that you can digest and understand it – before applying it to your current situation. There is a real risk of experiencing information overload, even though this is not my intent. There is just no escaping the fact that you need to have a high level of detailed information if you are going to be able to develop a plan that is comprehensive and realistic.

The most telling symptom of information overload is procrastination. So, if you find yourself putting the book down and then finding reasons to avoid "picking it back up," for now. Ask yourself, which information is causing you concern and perhaps consider moving forward to the next chapter and then moving back to the information that was blocking you. Here are some suggestions to help you manage the amount of content you are about to be exposed to:

- Make sure that you are reading this when you have decent energy reserves.
- Do not try to take in too much content in one sitting – pace yourself!
- If a section or concept is not clear to you, try leaving it and move to the next concept – come back to it after

you have had a chance for your brain to process the information

- Take notes. Often, when writing down information, we are able to process and understand information that was confusing when simply reading it
- Set up a schedule to complete this section, eg; a dedicated time & duration each week such as, every Tuesday and Thursday for 90 minutes.

I have also created a workbook, specifically for this section of the book, as an aid to allow you to take notes on the more involved concepts I unpack in this section. You can download your copy from the resources area of the support website (www.whencaniretire.com.au).

The structure of a book requires information to be presented in a linear form, so page twelve follows page eleven, which follows page ten and so on. You are going to find that developing your plan will not exactly follow that structure.

Yes, you will start the process in a step by step manner. However, as you progress through those steps it is likely that ideas, challenges, details and the like will pop into your head that will cause you to have to backtrack or leap forward to other sections of the plan so as to incorporate these thoughts. That is perfectly natural – frustrating sometimes, but natural. The planning process is all about gathering your thoughts and setting them out in a way that makes sense. Our minds do not always follow that process, so expect quite a bit of to-ing and fro-ing. In the end, that back and forth will result in a comprehensive plan that will provide you with the roadmap you are going to need.

Your plan needs to incorporate where you are now – from a career, social and financial perspective. You will need to identify where you want to be two, five, seven or more years from now and why. Understand that there are going to be roadblocks – obstacles that could get in the way of you achieving your goals and, along with these, some ideas as to what you can do to eliminate or minimise these and, in a worst case scenario, your plan B (C, D, E, F and more if necessary).

You will need to weigh up the risks you have identified and establish what (if anything) you might need to do about those. Finally, you will need to formalise an action plan – a step by step blueprint of the actions you will need to take to move you towards the achievement of your goals. These things (and a few more besides) are what I am going to unpack for you in this section of the book – and I'll be sure to include some handy tools that will support your efforts in all of these areas. Oh, and one more thing, you can also use these processes and tools to retire early! Why wait three, five or ten years to enjoy a life of your choosing?

I was fifty six when my wife and I started to contemplate our two year "adventure" to Germany and retirement was only just starting to be more than a "blip" on my radar and yet this event has changed both of our lives for the better and for good!

If the last five years has taught me anything it is that, If I can do this, anyone with a vision for a better future, along with some old fashioned determination and application, can do it. The time to start is now!

Walk Before You Run

"Every step of life shows much caution is required."
Johann Wolfgang von Goethe

As you begin exploring the possibilities of your retirement years you are going to get excited at the prospect of all of the things that you consider. In that process you are likely to be faced with the temptation to accelerate your plans – to jump in, to start sooner. After all, planning for your future should be exciting. However, whilst I am a firm believer that a plan without action will achieve nothing, action without at least some caution is likely to lead to disaster. Let's face it, when you are in your fifties and sixties you do not have the economic "wriggle" room to recover from disaster in the same way that you had in your younger years. Take my journey (thus far) as a case in point.

My wife and I were discussing our options in 2012 for our next five year plan. If anyone would have told me that, from this, we would be moving overseas I would have told them, "no way!" The conversation we had in mid-2012 birthed the idea that a move overseas for two years was an option - but it took some further investigation before we reached a decision at the beginning of 2013 that the move was feasible. We spent another twelve months developing that plan – basically going through all of the steps that this section of the book is going to take you through – before we were ready to take our first, tentative, steps to put the plan into action. It was a further eighteen months after that before we engaged our final steps in the plan to make the move the reality it became - when we boarded our flight for Frankfurt in late July 2015.

Admittedly we had the benefit of an inbuilt "brake" which acted as a restraint against us moving sooner and that was our daughter, Jasmine's, completion of her high school education at the end of 2014. Even with this, there were other elements of the plan that we could not have completed earlier, such as my securing my Australian Citizenship (government always moves at its own pace) and the economic realities of shifting the focus of my then business (I had certain contractual obligations to uphold for one).

Believe me, there were times that we got so excited at the prospect of the move that we wished we could do it sooner – so the temptation was most definitely there! That is how I know that you will be faced with similar temptations. Hopefully you will have some fixed points or "brakes" in your plan's scope to assist you in slowing down your desire to move quicker. If not, you are simply going to have to rigorously apply some of the principles of self-management we discussed in section one. To be perfectly honest, establishing (or revisiting) your plans for your "retirement" will take a decent amount of time if you apply the principles I have already outlined and will expand further upon as the book unfolds before you.

My journey began with that initial conversation with my wife in 2012 – this is where we established our goal. When I worked in the tourism and hospitality industry one of my mentors drummed into me that you always start with the end in mind and work backwards from there in developing your plan.

If you are in the enviable position of having plenty of time to consider your retirement lifestyle plan and its execution, as my wife and I were when we started planning for our two year "adventure", you have the luxury of being able to consider your options carefully – whether that be for a two, five, ten years or longer window.

But what if circumstances have forced you into a major lifestyle review? Covid19 is one example of this, where the impacts of an unforeseen event have catapulted you into a whole world of uncertainty which requires drastic and immediate action – you simply do not have the luxury of being able to sit back and meticulously put a plan together!

There are a lot of people who now find themselves in such a position, so this next chapter is especially for you and anyone who wants or needs to accelerate their process.

Ready Or Not – Retirement Here I Come

"I can teach anybody how to get what they want out of life. The problem is that I can't find anybody who can tell me what they want. Once you are crystal clear about the intended end result that you seek to produce, all the ways that it can become a done deal start to reveal themselves to you."
Mark Twain

Covid19 has a lot to answer for! Its impacts are going to be felt for many years to come but it is not the only event that has rocked the world and changed it forever. The Global Financial Crisis of 2008 and the destruction of the Twin Towers in New York (often referred to as "nine eleven") in 2001 are recent examples of events that have re-shaped our world. Then there are events that have a dramatic but more localised impact, such as; natural disasters (floods, fires, cyclones/hurricanes, etc.), man made events (nuclear and other major infra-structure accidents, wars, riots, local economy melt downs, etc.).

Unfortunately, life is full of uncertainty and there is always the possibility that circumstances, outside of our direct control, will put us in situations that we had not foreseen but that we have to do some-thing about – and quickly!

If you are to become a person that is in control of your life you need to accept the philosophy that it is not what happens to you but what you do about it that matters most. It is quite natural to, at first, regret what has happened to you but you must never allow yourself to focus on that – you cannot change what has happened but you can change what happens next, so that needs to be where you put your energies.

The Grief Cycle

The most important thing to do when you find yourself in circumstances you were not ready for – but must do something about – is to remain as calm as possible. You are not going to be able to achieve anything if you remain in a heightened emotional state or "panic" mode. No matter how drastic your situation may be there is a way through it and out of it.

At some point in everyone's life, there are going to be circumstances of such dramatic impact that they result in feelings of grief. In this book we are exploring this in relation to changes in our lifestyle that are forced upon us when we are not prepared for them – loss of job, total change of career, negative financial impacts, etc.

This type of grief is no less traumatic than that resulting from the death of a loved one, the end of a significant relationship, or any other change that alters life as you know it. In 1969, a Swiss-American psychiatrist named Elizabeth Kübler-Ross wrote in her book, "On Death and Dying", that grief could be divided into five stages. Her observations came from years of working with terminally ill individuals.

Her theory of grief became known as the Kübler-Ross model. While it was originally devised for people who were ill, these stages of grief have been found to apply for other experiences with loss, too. The five stages of grief is probably the most widely known but it's far from the only stages of grief theory. Several others exist as well, including ones with seven stages and ones with just two.

For our purposes the Kübler-Ross model is the one I will be featuring. Those five stages are:

- Denial
  This isn't happening, this can't be real are typical thoughts in this stage
- Anger
  How could they let this happen! Why is this happening to

me?! This isn't right! Are all typical responses during this stage

- Bargaining

  In this stage you are likely to find yourself creating a lot of "what if" and "if only" statements. Religious people will pray and make deals like "if you help me with this I will (insert offer)"

- Despair/Depression

  This can be difficult and messy. It can feel overwhelming. You may feel foggy, heavy, and confused. This may feel like the inevitable landing point of any loss. However, if you feel stuck here or can't seem to move past this stage of grief, talk with a trusted friend or mentor. In prolonged cases seek out the counsel of a mental health expert. A therapist can help you work through this period of coping. Typical thoughts include; I just can't see a way forward, why is this happening to me and why bother at all?

- Acceptance

  Acceptance is not necessarily a happy or uplifting stage of grief. It doesn't mean you've moved past the grief or loss. What it does mean is that you've accepted it and have come to understand what it means in your life now. You may feel very different in this stage. That's entirely expected. You've had a major change in your life which is likely to change the way you feel about many things. Look to acceptance as a way to see that there may be more good days than bad, but there may still be bad — and that's OK.

Not everyone will experience all five stages, and you may not go through them in this order. Grief is different for every person, so you may begin coping with loss in the bargaining stage and find yourself in anger or denial next. You may remain for months in one of the five stages but skip others entirely.

I have included the grief cycle details in order to help you better understand yourself. If you can identify your feelings at any given point in time and accept that everyone goes through the same process – albeit at differing paces and not necessarily in the same order – it will help you to be able to move forward quicker. It's not about supressing your emotions or about pretending that you do not have feelings over whatever event or circumstance.

It's about accepting that what has happened has happened but not allowing your feelings of grief to prevent you from taking positive steps to recover from the impact and shock, in order that you can continue to work towards improving your situation – as difficult as that may at first appear.

Accelerated Planning

One of the best ways to stimulate yourself to move as quickly as you can through the grief cycle is to take action. This is not to say that you "do stuff" just for the sake of being busy to take your mind off things. It's about taking action that will contribute to your road to recovery from the situation that is causing you stress.

Taking the right action will provide you with a stronger sense of control and the right action to take is that of an accelerated planning process. With this accelerated process your immediate goal is to achieve a position where the impacts of the event/circumstance are minimised, ending up in a position where more longer term plans can be formulated and engaged.

Typically, an accelerated plan will have a far shorter horizon than any full blown retirement lifestyle plan. Whereas your longer term plan may have an end date five or ten years away, your accelerated plan is going to be focused on the next six to twelve months – perhaps eighteen months at the absolute limit.

Adopting this approach provides you with a number of advantages:

- You are able to concentrate on the here and now
- The planning process is dramatically shortened
- You can focus on immediate priorities
- You can quickly identify and harness your resources

- You can identify a "light at the end of a shortened tunnel"

You are still going to need to engage in all of the steps outlined in this section of the book to complete your accelerated plan and you should also evaluate your risks but your goals are going to be few and short term.

In military terms you would refer to the accelerated plan as a "battle plan" whereas your long term lifestyle plan would be a "war plan". You can lose a few battles and still win the war!

If you do need to adopt an accelerated planning process, I have included an accelerated planning template in the resources area of the support website. (www.whencaniretire.com.au).

Accelerated plan or not you should always start planning with the end in mind. That is where I suggest you start – at the end. Ask yourself where you need to be in six, twelve or eighteen months from now? This becomes your primary goal and that is what we are going to deal with next – goals and how to set them so that you actually get there!

Knowing Where You Want To Be

"If what you are doing is not moving you towards your goals, then it's moving you away from them".
Brian Tracy

Whenever I think about effective goal setting, I think about the conversation between Alice and The Cheshire Cat in Lewis Carrol's Alice In Wonderland…

"Would you tell me, please, which way I ought to go from here?" asked Alice.

"That depends a good deal on where you want to get to," said the Cat.

"I don't much care where—" said Alice.

"Then it doesn't matter which way you go," said the Cat.

"—so long as I get somewhere," Alice added as an explanation.

"Oh, you're sure to do that," said the Cat, "if you only walk long enough."

Truly successful people do not, with few exceptions, experience success by accident. You are embarking on a crucial part of your life's journey. If you want this part of your life to deliver on your desires

133

and dreams you are going to have to plan your journey – and plan it well. For any journey to be successfully completed you need three core elements:

1. The desired destination
2. The starting point
3. A method to get from one to the other

Your desired destination is what your goal(s) represent – but before you go rushing off and setting your goals, let's make sure that your goals are actually goals and not just some aspirational statements that are never likely to eventuate. We all have a future focus, to one extent or another – we all have wishes and dreams. If you want to make any of these come true, you have to turn them into goals. Unfortunately, there are far too many people under the misapprehension that wishes, dreams and goals are the same thing – they're not! And what separates them is that goals are not just aspirational – they actually have a call to action built in.

Let me explain......

What moves a wish or a dream into becoming a goal are five key elements. These are:

1. It is Specific.

The goal must be clear and well defined. Vague or generalised goals don't work because they don't provide sufficient direction. Goals should show you the way.

2. It is Measurable.

You have to be able to measure your degree of success – how else will you know that you are on track? Ask yourself "How will I know when I have achieved this goal?" The answer to that question needs be in your goal statement.

3. It is Achievable.

Make sure that it's possible to achieve the goals you set. If you set a goal that you have no hope of achieving, you will only demoralise yourself and erode your confidence. Just make sure that the goal isn't too easy – you want it to stretch you just a little.

4. It is Relevant.

Each goal should be relevant to the direction you need to be heading in to accomplish your plan – which is to have a retirement that provides you with the quality of life you are aiming for.

5.   It is Time Sensitive.

All goals must have a "Use by" date! This deadline provides a sense of urgency which will encourage you to act.

These elements are often referred to as SMART goals – so, from this point on, make sure that all of your goals are SMART. Also, when you set your goals make sure that they motivate you. A great way to achieve that is to make sure that they are important to you, and that there is value in achieving them. If you have little interest in the outcome, or they lose significance in the bigger picture, then it is likely that you will not put in the work to make them happen - motivation is key to achieving goals.

It's fine to have multiple goals – just make sure that they don't compete with each other i.e.; the working on the achievement of one goal should not prevent you from achieving others. Just don't have too many!

It is highly likely that, at the beginning of this process, you will have a larger number of goals than you really need. So, have a look at your list and assign priorities to your goals. Consider dropping the low priority ones or incorporating them in one of your higher priority goals. Alternately, develop a sub classification of your goals into time periods e.g.; next six months, twelve months, next 36 months, next 60 months, etc (short, medium and long term)

We all only have a certain amount of energy and resource and you do not want to go wasting these on low priority goals or to be working on a long term goal when you should be focused on a short term one. Finally, record all of your goals – write them down or input them into your computer. The physical act of writing down a goal makes it more real and tangible. It's also harder to forget it, as well as impossible for your brain to play tricks on you if you try to rely on memory. Unless you have been used to setting goals – either in your career or personally – you are going to find this process tough to begin with, even though it may seem pretty straightforward.

After coaching literally thousands of people in this area over the last twenty years, I can tell you that what most people struggle with in this process are the elements of making the goal measurable and time sensitive. These two elements are what provides a goal with "bite". They also are what make a goal a little scary! You can access a goal setting template in the resources area of the support website at (www.whencaniretire.com.au).

Of course, any goal is going to require a set of actions which will be required to be undertaken if the goal is to be achieved. I will be running through that process with you a little later in this section of the book. For now, it's time to reflect on what your present situation is. Let's explore that in the next chapter.

Knowing Where You Are

*"It is better to have your head in the clouds and know where you are...
than to breathe the clearer atmosphere below them and think that you
are in paradise."*
Henry David Thoreau

Having set your goals, you have established your destination but
before you can head off on your journey to get there, you need to
know where you are starting from. Your starting point – "Ground
zero", so to speak, is where you are now. If you do not have an accurate (or honest) picture of where you are right now it is very likely that
whatever plan you develop will fail and this is a key point. It is all
well and good to "sweeten" the truth when people ask you how you
are doing or if everything is alright – we all want others to believe that
we are doing better than we really are.

It is this motivation that contributes, in part, to the massive popularity of social media – people can project an image of the sort of life
they dream about, as opposed to their present reality. However, you
should not be "sweetening" the truth when you are undertaking an assessment of yourself or establishing your starting point with your partner, spouse or close family members. This can be really difficult for
some – mainly because they are not living their desired life but one
that, through a procession of less than optimum choices, they currently
find themselves enduring. No matter where you currently are, you
need to be brutally honest with yourself when establishing your starting point. Look at this part of the process as a type of personal audit.
A chance to lay all of your cards (no matter how poor the deal has

been for you thus far) in front of you, so as to ascertain how far you have to travel in order to reach your desired destination.

Successful businesses conduct audits on a regular basis as this provides them with a "health check" as to how closely the business plan is matching the reality of the world around them. Audits help keep them on course - at the very least, they illustrate that a change of course might be required.

Whilst the news an audit delivers may not always be easy to swallow, you are far better to know where you are, and be able to take remedial action, before your situation becomes so dire that recovery is almost impossible. If you are not where you would have liked to be, this is a great opportunity to start to do something about that.

If you are where you would like to be – but are wanting to improve on that for your retirement years, this is where you start to take more control of what happens next. Your "audit" needs to incorporate pretty much every detail about your current situation. Consider elements such as;

- A Financial health check – what are your assets versus your liabilities? Your income(s) versus your expenditure(s)?
- What is your current mortgage? If you are renting, how much are you paying?
- What insurance cover do you currently have?
- Are you a member of a private health fund (as you get older this becomes more important)?
- How is your superannuation looking – should you be contributing more (if so, how much)? Are there tax benefits available that you are not taking advantage of?
- Where do you currently spend your income (can any of this expenditure be reduced or eliminated – what would the impact of this be)?
- Family situation – married or in a long term relationship? Single? Do you have children – are they

dependant on you for financial support? Do you have close family members that could be impacted by your decisions (eg; parents, siblings, etc)

- What is your employment situation – how long have you been in your current position? How secure is your role? Do you enjoy your job? Is your employer in good financial shape? Etc
- What pastimes are you involved in – what do these cost? Do any have the capacity to impact negatively on your health (e.g.; through injury or stress)? How much time do you currently allocate to these?
- What do you really enjoy doing (hobbies, interests, etc)? Why do you enjoy these?
- What do you do currently that you don't enjoy? How can you stop these? What will be the impact if you do? How will you deal with those (impacts)?
- What would you like to do more of and what would you like to do less of?

I'm sure that you are getting the picture! If you are anything like me, I had to go through this list a few times before I was satisfied that my list was comprehensive enough. My wife and I compiled our lists independently of each other and then compared the results. This helped us avoid the "group think" syndrome where you both end up missing the same things (when you work on the list together).

In section one of the book I urged caution when relying on the opinions of experts to make your decisions. That being said, I would urge you to seek the advice of financial experts for this part of your planning process. It's not so much their opinion you need here but their expertise on matters that the average person is just not up to date with. Who can keep up with all the ongoing changes to taxation law – especially when it comes to superannuation? Additionally, budgeting and financial planning is something that most of us do only a few times (and then, often, poorly) -whereas your accountant or financial adviser is doing this sort of thing on a daily basis. They also have the advantage of not being emotionally attached to the results and so are in a better position to provide objective assessment.

This personal audit process is, in effect, what is referred to in the business world as a "Situation Analysis". It is both a complex and critical task – fortunately, our friends in the business community have developed a few tools to aid in the process. Let me share some of these with you now.

SWOT Analysis

The acronym stands for **S**trengths, **W**eaknesses, **O**pportunities, **T**hreats and is a strategic planning technique you can use to help you identify strengths, weaknesses, opportunities, and threats related to your situation. It is designed to assist you with your decision-making processes – you can apply it to ask and answer questions which will generate meaningful information in each of the four categories. Whilst it does have its limitations, it is a great starting point when undertaking a personal plan – such as the one you will need to complete if you are to achieve the sort of lifestyle in retirement that you desire.

Strengths: The characteristics, qualities and resources that provide you with an advantage in terms of achieving your plan's goals.

Weaknesses: The characteristics qualities and resources (or lack thereof) that could place your plan in jeopardy.

Opportunities: The elements in the environment that you could exploit to your advantage - in terms of the achieving your plan's goals.

Threats: The elements in the environment that could cause you trouble in terms of the achieving your plan's goals.

Strengths and weakness are frequently internally related ie; you have control over their impact/continuation. Identifying these is not difficult – although it can be confronting when you start to honestly appraise your weaknesses. On the other hand, opportunities and threats commonly focus on the external environment i.e.; you have little control over their existence (but do have a degree of control over what you decide to do about them). Establishing a comprehensive and accurate list of these requires some broad based thinking – as well as some "out of the box" thinking (for things that may not be an issue at this point in time but could be in the future). There's a very useful tool that will assist you with these and it is called a PESTEL analysis.

There's a SWOT analysis template in the resources area of the website. (www.whencaniretire.com.au)

PESTEL Analysis

This is an excellent broad, fact-finding tool which will help you identify the external factors that could impact on your decisions as they relate to your goals and your action plan going forward (more on that action plan shortly). As an individual you cannot affect these factors, but they can significantly affect you. PESTEL is an acronym of the factors that the tool addresses – **Political, Economic, Social, Technological, Environmental, Legal.**

Political Factors: Explores to what degree government activity could influence or impact your plan - government policy, political stability or instability, corruption, tax policy, etc.

Economic Factors: Economic factors will impact you plans – it's just a question of to what extent. Factors include economic growth, exchange rates, inflation rates, interest rates, etc.

Social Factors: What changes in social and cultural expectations could impact on your plan? Consider elements such as; population growth rate, age distribution (especially the "Age Wave" previously discussed), health consciousness, lifestyle attitudes, cultural shifts, etc.

Technological Factors: We already know the impact that technology is having today – how will this shape your tomorrow? Elements to consider include; technology innovations, automation, artificial intelligence (AI), technological change, etc

Environmental Factors: We are all more than aware of the Climate Change debate – whether you are a supporter or not, this issue will deliver changes in our society. Environmental factors have come to the forefront in society only relatively recently. They may especially affect industries such as tourism, farming, agriculture and insurance. How could they impact on your goals?

Legal Factors: This factor has considerable overlap with the political factors (as government introduces new legislation). You need to know what is and what is not legal in order to action your plan successfully and ethically.

There's a PESTEL analysis template in the resources area of the website. (www.whencaniretire.com.au)

As you are no doubt starting to realise, establishing a clear and accurate picture of where you are now is quite an involved and time consuming business. This is as it should be – establishing your starting point accurately is critical to your success. After all, if you get your starting point wrong you are going to be struggling to reach your destination. As Jim Rohn, a very well-known and respected American business philosopher and motivational speaker once said;

"I find it fascinating that most people plan their vacations with better care than they plan their lives. Perhaps that is because escape is easier than change."

If you don't think and plan in advance, you can easily end up being angry, frustrated, and not satisfied with your life; because everything that follows is so reliant on getting this first element right do not be either afraid or concerned to spend what would appear to be a disproportionate amount of time (in comparison to the whole process) on it. In the words of Albert Einstein;

"If I had an hour to solve a problem, I'd spend 55 minutes thinking about the problem and five minutes thinking about solutions."

In this case you definitely have more than an hour available to you – but I'm sure you get the point Once you have your starting point documented and you are satisfied that it is accurate, it is time to start thinking about how you intend to reach that destination but before you do that, you need to understand why you are doing this – and that reason may not be what you think it is. That is what we will address in the next chapter – let's go and uncover your "Why"

Discovering Your Why

"If we want to feel an undying passion in our lives, if we want to feel we are contributing to something bigger than ourselves, we all need to know our WHY."
Simon Sinek

When you get used to other people making decisions that impact your life it can easily become a habit. Think about it, when you were growing up your parents made most of life's decisions for you – even as you grew older, left high school and either went to university or entered the workforce, they still had a huge influence on the decisions you made early on in your adult life.

For most of your working life decisions are being made for you – by your line manager and the hierarchy of the organisation. Your life outside of work is often driven by circumstances rather than by design – buying your first home, starting your own family and then supporting that family. What are you going to do now that you have reached a stage in your life where your family responsibilities are changing (your children are forging their own paths) and you are not in the workforce?

Here, again, is where your mindset (which I covered in section one of the book) is going to have to change – the way you make your decisions needs to change and, for a lot of people, this is a very challenging time. When approaching or entering your retirement years you need to reassess your decision making processes because the criteria you have been using up until this point no longer apply.

For a long, long time the drivers that stimulate your decision making have been external – often referred to as being "extrinsic". This has been the situation for so long that you do not even think about it – it seems totally natural.

Here are some examples of what they may look like;

- Your employer offers you a promotion. It comes with a substantial pay increase, but it does mean moving to another city
- Your child is offered a scholarship at a prestigious high school which would require a move across town
- The company you work for is acquired by a competitor and a restructure means your job role is going to change substantially
- Your partner/spouse has mentioned that they would like to upgrade their qualifications which will require full time study for twelve months

These are just a small selection of the types of extrinsic forces that shape the decisions we make or act as a catalyst for substantial change in our lives. As you approach and enter retirement many (if not all) of these extrinsic forces no longer apply. So, now you are going to need to move to providing your own impetus for decision making. You need to become proactive in this space – where you are deciding your next moves in order for you to achieve what you have established as being your goals. This is often referred to as "intrinsic" - you provide your impetus as opposed to an external entity or situation.

This is where understanding your "why" becomes crucial. If you know and understand your "why" you will have the necessary, drive and energy to forge ahead – even when the tide may be running against you. Your "why" fuels your passion and your passion provides you with energy. In retirement you need this drive, otherwise you will simply drift along, being bounced around by life's continual hiccups and end up withering away as a result. This is not how retirement is meant to be!

Now, don't get me wrong – I am not suggesting that you attack your retirement like a bull in a china shop, charging this way and that! Maintaining that sort of energy is hard work and you have been working hard for too long as it is! You do not need to always be "on" in retirement. However, all of us do need to have a purpose, it's what gives our lives meaning.

The power of purpose cannot be underestimated - a clear sense of purpose enables you to focus your efforts on what matters most, compelling you to take (calculated) risks and push forward regardless of the odds or obstacles.

Unlike animals, which are driven simply to survive, we humans crave more from life than just survival. Without purpose we can quickly fall into disillusionment, distraction and a quiet sense of despair.

One of the world's most recognised advocates for the importance of understanding your "why" is Simon Sinek - a British author and speaker. His vision is to "live in a world where the vast majority of us wake up inspired, feel safe at work and return home fulfilled at the end of the day". Look him up on YouTube, he is a captivating speaker and what he says makes absolute sense – especially when intrinsic motivation becomes important, as it is when we exit the mainstream workforce.

You may be thinking that this is all well and good but that you already have your retirement sorted – you're going to take it easy, finally get to do all those things you have never had the time for and generally enjoy life. Yes, there are a lot of people who feel the same way and, for the first few years of retirement they do exactly that. It doesn't take long, though, for the gloss to wear off that world. By all means, kick back and relax for a while - one year, two, three. You have worked hard and had a lot of disappointments; you deserve a break. But please, think about what happens after that – because you will reach a point where you become bored or you just get this feeling that "something" is missing from your life.

That's when knowing your "why" is going to make the difference between a life with purpose and focus versus a life with this constant nagging feeling that something is missing. While there's no one method for discovering your life's purpose, there are many ways you can gain deeper insight into yourself, and a larger perspective on what it is that you have to offer the world.

Four Questions To Ask Yourself

Here are four questions that will help you start on the journey to find your "why" – and lead you to discovering the balance between what you care about, what you can contribute, and what will be valued most.

1. When do you feel most alive?

When you are working toward things that inspire you, it literally makes you feel more alive. This is not about taking your dream holiday or attending your favourite artist's music concert. It's bigger than that – in fact, it's bigger than you! It's about connecting with what you're passionate about, knowing that when you focus your attention on endeavours that light a fire inside you, you grow both your impact and influence in ways that nothing else can. This is about you connecting to a cause that's bigger than you are, but which is also congruent with who you are and what you care about.

2. What are your natural strengths?

In his book "The Element", Sir Ken Robinson says that our "element" is the point at which natural talent and skill meets personal passion. When we are in our element, we are not only more productive - we add more value and enjoy more personal and professional fulfilment. Often, it's also often where we can also make more money!

What are the things you've always been good at (sometimes wondering why others find it so hard)? Do you see solutions where others see problems? Are you creative, able to think "outside the box"? Are you brilliant in the details, naturally good at executing projects with a precision that others lack? You can also be passionate about things you have no natural talent for, and talented at things for which you hold little passion. In my experience I have found that we rarely aspire toward ambitions we have no natural talent to achieve.

3. Where do you add the greatest value?

Doing things that you're good at, but which you loathe, is not a pathway to fulfilment. Let's face it, most of us have been doing that for much of our working lives! That said, knowing your greatest strengths and where you can add the most value—through the application of your education, skills, knowledge and experience—can help you focus on the opportunities where you are most likely to succeed and therefore find the greatest sense of accomplishment and contribution. Don't be afraid though to attempt to take on new challenges – you may not excel in the short term but, over time, you'll get better and, if you stick at it, achieve mastery. After all, in retirement, the need to be productive -quickly- is not as great. Ask yourself what you're well placed and equipped to help solve in your community. You can also ask yourself what problems you really enjoy solving, and what problems you feel passionate about trying to solve. You'll then be more successful at focusing on your natural strengths and those things you're innately good at.

4. How will you measure your life?

As the American statesman, Alexander Hamilton once said, "people who don't stand for something, can easily fall for anything". How you want to measure your life means making a stand for something and then living your life in alignment with that. To live with purpose means focusing on things that matter most (to you). During our working lives most of us are not in a position to trade the security of a regular wage in order to pursue our passion. But once we retire that is no longer the case. Now we have an opportunity to follow our heart – what that means for you is going to be different to what it means to me. This is a deeply personal aspect of our lives but a very important one.

More than anything, knowing your "why" will provide you with a compass that will assist you in making the right decisions as to your direction and action in what should be the most fulfilling part of your time on this planet. It may also compel you to take on challenges that will stretch you as much as they inspire you. Time now, perhaps, to revisit the goals you set earlier – do they align with your "why"? Once you are satisfied that this is this case, you are going to need to establish what might get in the way of you achieving your goals Let's look at how you can identify your potential obstacles.

Dealing With Obstacles

"Obstacles are necessary for success because, with anything important, victory comes only after many struggles and countless defeats".
Og Mandino

According to German Field Marshal Rommel, "no plan survives contact with the enemy" This thinking also applies to goals – "no goal is ever achieved without overcoming obstacles"

Obstacles are like a landmine which stands between you and your goals. People often give up on their goals as a direct result of experiencing obstacles. They either didn't see the obstacle coming or expected to simply walk through their plan without any hiccups occurring. Trust me when I say that every goal we set comes with an array of landmines and these landmines typically manifest as problems that we must figure out how to overcome.

The moment you establish a goal you are, by default, setting yourself up to experience some set-backs – obstacles that are going to make achieving your goal more difficult than you originally imagined. Sometimes they might even make you consider that the goal is impossible! However, if we accept that obstacles are a natural part of the process, what we come to realise is that, by identifying what obstacles we are likely to face in advance, we are better positioned to be able to deal with them and achieve our goal.

The Three Types of Obstacles You Will Encounter

There are three types of obstacles that you will likely face as you implement you plan - personal, environmental, and social. Each of these three presents you with a different set of challenges. Get through these challenges, and you will make inroads into your goal. Wilt in the face of these challenges and your goal will always remain out of reach.

1. Personal Obstacles

Personal obstacles are related to our psychology, behaviour, and state-of-mind. They typically include;

- Unhelpful habits
- Debilitating emotions
- Paralyzing fears
- Limiting beliefs.

The reason these obstacles prevent us from moving forward comes down to how we choose to interpret events and circumstances, and the subsequent thoughts we choose to dwell upon. These thoughts prevent us from making objective decisions. The resulting poor choices lead us down less than optimal paths as we work toward our goals. You must first learn to effectively control your thoughts before you apply the ideas presented here.

Here is a list of personal obstacles that could prevent you from achieving your goals:

Lack of pain	Lack of patience
Lack of knowledge	Lack of inspiration
Lack of skill	Fear of change
Feeling unworthy	Procrastination
Language Patterns	Disorganization
Time constraints	Complacency
Too many excuses	Always complaining
Lack of discipline	Lack of desire and passion
Fear of failure	Perfectionism

Pessimistic thoughts Lack of urgency

Not taking responsibility

Take a moment to identify if any of these obstacles are familiar to you

Ask yourself:

- Which of these personal obstacles do I typically succumb to?
- How exactly are these obstacles manifesting in my life? What are the triggers?
- Why exactly do I tend to succumb to these obstacles? When? Where? At what specific times?
- How are these obstacles preventing me from achieving my goals?
- How can I begin working through these obstacles?

2. Social Obstacles that Could Get in Your Way

Social obstacles are related to people who either do not cooperate with you, sabotage you or are merely incompetent and unable to fulfil the responsibilities required of them.

When it comes to social obstacles, it's essential to do a little forward planning to ensure that you can communicate requirements unambiguously. It also helps to develop good strong bonds and relationships with the people you rely on most.

Ask yourself:

- Whose support do I need to achieve my goals?
- Who is currently holding me back from this? How?
- Is it possible to mend or change this relationship and realign this person to my goals?
- How can I build more supportive relationships with the people in my life?

The key here is to subtly influence people by attempting to better understand their needs, motives, and desires. In other words, how does helping you (achieve your goals) help them (achieve their goals)? Only in this way will you successfully improve your chances of manoeuvring through the social obstacles in your life.

3. Environmental Obstacles

Environmental obstacles are often unexpected conditions and circumstances that you often have very little control over. Because environmental obstacles are often unexpected occurrences, we are frequently ill-prepared and unable to deal with them effectively. However, with a little research and forward planning, you can set in place contingency plans that can help you work through these obstacles in more effective ways. To do this, begin by exploring Murphy's Law.

Murphy's Law states that anything that can go wrong, will go wrong at the worst possible time - all of the time when you least expect it. (Some people believe that Murphy was an optimist!) The PESTEL analysis tool that I introduced earlier is a great way to identify potential obstacles

Overcoming Obstacles

When it comes to overcoming obstacles, many people just don't know what to do, where to begin or how to move forward when they hit one of these landmines – especially when they believe they are, in fact, in a minefield!

Rather than facing that struggle to start over again or falling into the emotional abyss of feeling that your goals and dreams seem to have fallen apart, you need to shift your thinking. The best way to do that is to ask yourself some questions;

- Question the problem
  - What are the indications that this is a problem for you?
  - How do you know this is accurate?
- Question the origins of the problem:
  - How did all this start?
  - Who or what perpetuates this problem?
- Identify the details of the problem:
  - When did it happen?
  - How did it happen?
  - Where did it happen?
- Explore the consequences of having this problem:
  - What would happen if you ignored it?
  - When could it become a bigger problem?
  - What could lead to this specific outcome?
  - How does this affect you/others?

- o How does this affect life?
- o Could resolving this cause other problems?
- Take control of your behaviour:
  - o What aspects of this problem can/can't you control?
  - o How could you adapt to all the things you can't control?
- Identify the things you would like to keep:
  - o What is happening that is good?
  - o What would you like to see continue to happen?
- Gain proper perspective on the situation:
  - o What are your assumptions about this?
  - o How are your assumptions contributing to the problem?
  - o What is another perspective you haven't considered?
  - o Who has successfully overcome this problem?
  - o What can you learn from this person to help you work through your problem?
- Expand your options:
  - o What could you do differently?
  - o Who could assist you along this journey toward solving this problem?
  - o Where haven't you looked for a solution?
  - o How will you know when this problem has been resolved?
  - o What is your criteria for success?

At the very least, what these questions will do is help you to see what lies behind the obstacles you currently face, and this will improve your ability to develop solutions. Of course, there are going to be situations where a strategy to deal with the obstacle eludes you –

especially if it has created a situation or issue you have little or no experience with.

These are the situations where, if the obstacle relates to a critical goal, you may want to seek out professional advice – and I do mean professional advice! Unless a friend or relative has direct experience in the area that is troubling you (and they have successfully dealt with it in the past) do not rely solely on their counsel. Uninformed advice is nothing more than opinion and everyone has plenty of these. By all means, seek out opinions that may differ from your own – they may well provide you with a perspective that aids you in reaching a solution.

However, unless you are certain about the opinion's validity, you are better to engage the services of a professional in the field. The cost of doing this is a wise investment – especially if a wrong decision could end up costing you thousands of dollars or worse.

Having identified potential obstacles you are going to need to develop some alternate actions by which you can overcome them, and this will require some "out of the box" thinking. That is what we are going to tackle next.

Thinking Creatively

"No problem can be solved from the same level of consciousness that created it."
Albert Einstein

It is all well and good to think about the obstacles you are likely to face on your journey towards a retirement lifestyle over which you exercise the bulk of control. However, developing strategies to deal with those obstacles is going to require you to expand your thinking beyond the level you employed to identify them. The pace of life today is unforgiving – we are having to make "on the spot" decisions far too quickly for most people's liking (& comfort). This pressure of pace tends to force us to be reactive rather than proactive.

The reactive space tends to focus on the here and now and this is mostly concerned with issues of a day to day nature. This "here and now" focus tends to become our default – because we are in that mode most of the time. Whilst this focus is necessary, it is not suited for all of our decision making & problem solving – it is certainly a poor option when it comes to making decisions about the medium to long term. If you are going to fully explore the potential that your retirement years presents you need to become more proactive and this requires a different level of thinking. Our brain is an unbelievably powerful tool but, like most tools, unless you use it correctly you are not going to get as much from it as you should.

We can process data thousands of times faster than even the most powerful computer (at this point!) – we absorb, analyse and then come up with a solution in milliseconds. Take the relatively simple day to day act of driving a motor vehicle; Not only are we making mathematical calculations (even those of us who claim to be poor at maths do this!) about our speed, trajectory and destination but we are also making similar calculations about those driving around us and opposite us, pedestrians on the sides of the road – even objects in our immediate air space.

Even with all of this going on, we still have enough processing capacity to be able to think about what we have on for that day and perhaps the rest of the week, listen to the radio and talk on our (hands free) mobile phones. Our processing capacity is awesome. Try doing all of that with your PC and all you will get is the blue screen of death, you know the one, "A critical error has occurred and you need to shut down your computer" – why is it that this only happens when you most need the PC?

Despite this processing power, our brains do have limitations. Most of the time, though, we think we have reached that limitation when we actually haven't. All we've done is not use our brain correctly but still expected it to give us the solution we have been looking for. Simply put, because we haven't ever really tried to understand the workings of our minds, we often try to use them in a way that limits our mind's capacity to deliver what has been asked of it. In a sense, our minds are similar to a PC (similar but definitely not the same) – what you put into them and the way you ask the question, will often determine your outcome.

Our brains are very complex, and a thorough understanding of the brain is a lifetime's work – many lifetime's work! Science is still trying to figure out how this wonderful organ operates. What we do know is that our brain's process data in one of two ways – analytically and creatively (we'll leave emotion out of the equation for now – even though it plays a huge role in our decision making).

The analytical function is well documented and is definitely the function we understand most about – more on this in a moment. The creative function is less well documented, but we understand enough about it to be able to make some interesting observations. For our purposes here, we are less concerned with how our brain's work than we are about how to use our brains more effectively. So, let's examine these two primary processes, Analytical and Creative thinking.

Analytical Thinking

We use analytical thinking to sort through issues in a reasoned, logical, approach – we take information and put it into a logical sequence. Hopefully, we have enough data for the sequence to make sense. Where there are a few gaps in the data we are able to bridge them, through analysis, to come up with a solution – and usually fairly quickly (once we have assembled enough data).

Our education system teaches us to think logically – especially mathematics and science. This type of thinking is convergent – it takes a collection of facts and, through a process of elimination, narrows down options until a solution is found. This type of thinking is also referred to as vertical thinking because there is one logical route which leads to the most appropriate answer. Unfortunately, there is a tendency for most of us to rely upon our analytical thinking processes too much. This is because we are most familiar with this process – after all, for most of our years spent being educated we were encouraged and taught to think analytically. The end result of that emphasis is that, because we have spent so much time thinking analytically, we are more comfortable with that process and so tend to rely it on more.

We make decisions every day and many of those decisions require analytical or critical thinking. We all have to make decisions that impact our friends, our bosses, peers and families. Surely, we want to make the best possible decisions to provide the best possible outcomes for these people? In that regard, can you become a better analytical thinker? You can, but it takes practice.

The first and most important step in analytical thinking is to recognise and acknowledge your own biases. We interpret all the information we receive through those filters (biases). Recognition of those biases will help you see the information from different viewpoints.

The second most important step may be to recognise the bias of those providing the information. Everyone is biased, (including you!). If you can remove or identify these biases, you can get closer to truth.

That may seem simple enough, but it isn't. Fortunately, there are processes you can use to improve your analytical thinking skills.

Next time you have to analyse a situation or problem try this process and see if it helps you reach a better decision:

1. Open mind

Skilled analytical thinking requires you to methodically break down problems, ideas or arguments into their constituent parts, in order to explain why they are 'The way they are'. Whether you agree with what is being presented isn't the point. Analytical thinking demands an unprejudiced and unbiased approach – including accepting the possibility that you may be wrong. Considering every viewpoint helps to achieve balance of thought.

2. Good reason

Objectivity is key. You must present reliable evidence, hard facts, and logical conclusions to convince others that you have properly evaluated a given situation. Inconsistent, missing, unsupported, or irrelevant information – as well as plain untruths – will indicate poor judgement on your part, and may even raise suspicions of vested interest or dubious motivation. Rationality is an essential tool for developing reasoned arguments.

3. Question

We first discussed this in section one – as a part of "Critical thinking. Ask questions relentlessly: who, what, when, where, why, how? Look beneath the surface. Establish the validity of any assumptions surrounding the main issues. Even investigate the credibility of those advancing certain arguments if required. Are emotional or subjective factors at play? What are the strengths and weaknesses of the points of view being expressed? Would these apply in all situations and if not, what allowances would have to be made? Leave no stone unturned.

Analytical thinking does have its limits – it will serve you well when you have a solid base of facts from which to start and not many gaps in the process. When you move from the known to the relatively unknown, analytical thinking can be very useful in navigating a course for you. Where we run into difficulties applying the analytical process is when we try to use it when the data is very sketchy or unreliable (perhaps heavily biased and we haven't recognised this) or when the situation is totally unknown to us – such as entering retirement. This is where creative thinking can help.

Creative Thinking

Creative thinking is very different from analytical thinking - it is not immediately concerned with looking for solutions. Instead, it looks for many ideas which may lead to possible solutions. Creative thinking is divergent – it goes in many different directions to look for possibilities. It is also referred to as lateral thinking (a term coined by the recognised master in the subject – Edward De Bono) because it may go in a direction which appears not to be toward the solution (sideways or around).

Creative thinking is well suited to dealing with situations where information is unreliable or scant and is especially useful when dealing with what is a largely unknown environment – dare I say it?? Such as in retirement. For most of us, creative thinking does not come easily – we are better at analytical thinking because this is what we have been taught and, because it is what we tend to do most of, we are more familiar with it. We have formed a thinking habit. However, we are all capable of creative thinking if we give it a little bit of conscious effort.

Creative thinking is both an ability and a skill. A simple definition is that creativity is the ability to imagine or invent something new. Creativity is not the ability to create out of nothing, but the ability to generate new ideas by combining, changing, or reapplying existing ideas. Innovation has its roots in thinking creatively. Some creative ideas are astonishing and brilliant, while others are just simple, good, practical ideas that no one seems to have thought of yet. Believe it or not, everyone has substantial creative ability. Just look at how creative children are. In adults, creativity has often been suppressed through education, but it is still there and can be reawakened. Often all that's needed to be creative is to make a commitment to creativity and to take the time for it.

Creativity is also an attitude: the ability to accept change and new-ness, a willingness to play with ideas and possibilities, a flexibility of outlook, the habit of enjoying the good, while looking for ways to im-prove it. We are socialised into accepting only a small number of per-mitted or normal things, like chocolate-covered strawberries, for example.

The creative person realises that there are other possibilities, like cheese and banana sandwiches, or chocolate-covered prunes! Creative people work hard (and continually) to improve ideas and solutions, by making gradual alterations and refinements to their works. Contrary to the mythology surrounding creativity, very, very few works of crea-tive excellence are produced with a single stroke of brilliance or in a frenzy of rapid activity.

Much closer to the real truth are the stories of companies who had to take the invention away from the inventor in order to market it be-cause the inventor would have kept on tweaking it and fiddling with it, always trying to make it a little better. The creative person knows that there is always room for improvement.

Several methods have been identified for producing creative re-sults. Here are five of the more common ones:

1. **Evolution**; This is the method of incremental improve-ment. New ideas stem from other ideas, new solutions from previous ones, the new ones slightly improved over the old ones. Many of the very sophisticated things we en-joy today developed through a long period of constant im-provement. Making something a little better here, a little better there gradually makes it something a lot better-- even entirely different from the original.

For example, consider the airplane - 21st Century commercial air-craft bear no resemblance to their early ancestors. Military jet fighters bear even less resemblance to their original counterparts. The evolu-tionary method of creativity also reminds us of that critical principle: Every problem that has been solved can be solved again in a better way.

Creative thinkers do not subscribe to the idea that once a problem has been solved, it can be forgotten, or to the notion that "if it isn't broke, don't fix it." A creative thinker's philosophy is that "there is no such thing as an insignificant improvement."

> 2. **Synthesis;** With this method, two or more existing ideas are combined into a third, new idea. Combining the ideas of a magazine and an audio tape gives the idea of a magazine you can listen to - one useful for blind people or commuters.

For example, popular radio show broadcasts are now often recorded and turned into "Podcasts" that listeners can download and replay at times that suit them.

> 3. **Revolution;** Sometimes the best new idea is a completely different one, a marked change from the previous ones. While an evolutionary improvement philosophy might cause a professor to ask, "how can I make my lectures better and better?" a revolutionary idea might be, "why not stop lecturing and have the students teach each other, working as teams or presenting reports?"

For example, the evolutionary technology in fighting termites eating away at houses has been to develop safer and faster pesticides and gasses to kill them. A somewhat revolutionary change has been to abandon gasses altogether in favour of liquid nitrogen, which freezes them to death or microwaves, which bake them. A truly revolutionary creative idea would be to ask, "How can we prevent them from eating houses in the first place?" A new termite bait that is placed in the ground in a perimeter around a house provides one answer to this question. Building the house frame using steel is another.

> 4. **Reapplication;** Look at something old in a new way. Go beyond labels. Un-fixate, remove prejudices, expectations and assumptions and discover how something can be reapplied. One creative person might go to the junkyard and see art in an old Ford model T transmission. He paints it

up and puts it in his living room. Another creative person might see in the same transmission the necessary gears for a multi-speed hot walker for his horse. He hooks it to some poles and a motor and puts it in his corral. The key is to see beyond the previous or stated applications for some idea, solution, or thing and to see what other application is possible.

For example, a paperclip can be used as a tiny screwdriver if filed down; paint can be used as a kind of glue to prevent screws from loosening in machinery; dishwashing detergents can be used to remove the DNA from bacteria in a lab; general purpose spray cleaners can be used to kill ants.

5. **Changing Direction;** Many creative breakthroughs occur when attention is shifted from one angle of a problem to another. This is sometimes called creative insight.

A classic example is that of the highway department trying to keep kids from skateboarding in a concrete-lined drainage ditch. The highway department put up a fence to keep the kids out; the kids went around it. The department then put up a longer fence; the kids cut a hole in it. The department then put up a stronger fence; it, too, was cut. The department then put a threatening sign on the fence; it was ignored.

Finally, someone decided to change direction, and asked, "What really is the problem here? It's not that the kids keep getting through the barrier, but that they want to skateboard in the ditch. So how can we keep them from skateboarding in the ditch?" The solution was to remove their desire by pouring some concrete in the bottom of the ditch to remove the smooth curve. The sharp angle created by the concrete made skateboarding impossible and the activity stopped. No more skateboarding problems, no more fence problems.

This example reveals a critical truth in problem solving: the goal is to solve the problem, not to implement a particular solution. When one solution path is not working, shift to another. There is no commitment to a particular path, only to a particular goal. Path fixation can sometimes be a problem for those who do not understand this; they become overcommitted to a path that does not work and only frustration results.

Myths about Creative Thinking and Problem Solving

1. Every problem has only one solution (or one right answer). The goal of problem solving is to solve the problem, and most problems can be solved in any number of ways. If you discover a solution that works, it is a good solution. There may be other solutions thought of by other people, but that doesn't make your solution wrong. What is THE solution to putting words on paper? Fountain pen, ball point, pencil, marker, typewriter, printer, Xerox machine, printing press?

2. The best answer/solution/method has already been found. Look at the history of any solution set and you'll see that improvements, new solutions, new right answers, are always being found. What is the solution to human transportation? The ox or horse, the cart, the wagon, the train, the car, the airplane, the jet? Is that the best and last? What about pneumatic tubes, hovercraft, even Star Trek type transporters (beam me up Scotty!)?

On a more everyday level, many solutions now seen as best or at least entrenched were put in place hastily and without much thought-- such as the use of drivers' licenses for ID cards. Other solutions are entrenched simply for historical reasons: they've always been done that way. Why do shoelaces still exist, when technology has produced several other, better ways to attach shoes to feet (like Velcro, elastic, snap buttons, and so on)?

3. Creative answers are complex technologically. Only a few problems require complex technological solutions. Most problems you'll meet with require only a thoughtful solution requiring personal action and perhaps a few simple tools. Even many problems that seem to require a technological solution can be addressed in other ways.

For example, what is the solution to the large percentage of packages ruined by the Post Office? Look at the Post Office package handling method. Packages are tossed in bins when you send them. For the solution, look at United Parcel. When you send a package, it is put on a shelf. The change from bin to shelf is not a complex or technological solution; it's just a good idea, using commonly available materials.

As another example, when hot dogs were first invented, they were served to customers with gloves to hold them. Unfortunately, the customers kept walking off with the gloves. The solution was not at all complex: serve the hot dog on a roll so that the customer's fingers were still insulated from the heat. The roll could be eaten along with the dog. No more worries about disappearing gloves. (Note by the way what a good example of changing direction this is. Instead of asking, "How can I keep the gloves from being taken?" the hot dog server stopped thinking about gloves altogether).

4. Ideas either come or they don't. The catch cry among the frustrated analytical thinkers is often, "nothing will help!" This is simply not true. There are many successful techniques for stimulating idea generation – you can access these in the resources section of the website. (www.whencaniretire.com.au)

Characteristics of Creative People

Everyone is creative but some are more creative than others. If you would like to become more creative than you currently are here are some characteristics to think about:

- Suspends judgment/sees problems as opportunities/challenges assumptions/ doesn't give up easily/comfortable with imagination/sees problems as interesting/curious/optimistic/enjoys challenge/seeks problems/perseveres/ works hard

When we need to problem solve – like in identifying solutions to obstacles, both kinds of thinking (Analytical and Creative) are important to us. First, we must analyse the problem; then we must generate possible solutions; next we must choose and implement the best solution; and finally, we must evaluate the effectiveness of the solution. As you can see, this process reveals an alternation between the two kinds of thinking, analytical and creative. In practice, both kinds of thinking operate together much of the time and are not really independent of each other.

For example; when Thomas Edison invented the light bulb, the idea of an incandescent light source was most definitely creative. However, the more than 1,000 times he tested the materials required to make the idea work was definitely an analytical process - with some of the materials used another example of creative thinking.

Whether you see yourself as a primarily analytical or creative thinker is not as important as accepting that, in order to be successful, you need to engage with both types and it is highly likely that, as you do this, you are going to face some barriers to achieving the level of thinking you need.

There is additional information on thinking barriers in the support website which you can access here: resources on

The nature of obstacles is that they are always going to get in your way. This does not have to result in disaster or the abandonment of your plans – provided you are prepared for them. Identifying obstacles and using appropriate thinking techniques to determine strategies to deal with them, will allow you to simply activate those strategies should the obstacle event actually occur. Remember, it is all about understanding your risks and being prepared for the change in your life that retirement represents – whether that change has been forced upon you by circumstances out of your control or whether it is just the next phase of your life approaching.

Facing change and responding appropriately to it is probably one of our biggest challenges, so let's explore what that might look like and how best to deal with it, when it comes to our retirement planning.

Change And Why Resistance Is Futile

"Progress is impossible without change, and those who cannot change their minds cannot change anything."
George Bernard Shaw

Change is at the very core of what this book is about – the first paragraph of the introduction is testament to that...

"It was the best of times, it was the worst of times, it was the age of wisdom, it was the age of foolishness, it was the epoch of belief, it was the epoch of incredulity, it was the season of Light, it was the season of Darkness, it was the spring of hope, it was the winter of despair, we had everything before us......"

Charles Dickens was addressing the alarming pace of change in the mid nineteenth century – it is, arguably, one of the reasons that "A Tale of Two Cities" continues to sell one hundred and fifty years later.

You have experienced change in your life and continue to do so – one of your biggest life changes is approaching you even as you read this (perhaps it is even upon you now) – retirement. It is only fitting that we discuss this phenomenon in light of that event. First allow me to share with you a definition of what change is. According to the Dictionary, "change" is defined as follows;

"A transformation or transition from one state, condition, or phase to another."

Change is something different than what existed previously (as we knew it). Your life in retirement is going to be different from your life in the workforce. Whether that change is for the better will depend entirely on you. One of the motivations for me writing this book was to provide people, like you, with information that will positively contribute to a retirement which provides a lifestyle that rewards you for your years of effort and sacrifice up to this point. That will not happen by accident and it certainly will not happen by resisting the changes that retirement brings with it. You simply must be prepared to take the bull by the horns and manage the changes you are faced with.

This means coordinating a number of activities and relationships so that you are in the best position to benefit from, the process of change – as it relates to your circumstances. The forces of change are largely manifested in external impacts and this is what the majority of people focus upon. However, change also applies to your mindset – which is why I included a chapter on mindset in section one of the book.

Change is coming for you and in a big way. Retirement will happen for you, sooner or later. You are far better to get on board with it sooner and be ready, than to be found scrambling around and trying to cope when it does finally arrive. For some that thought is quite comforting but for many it is absolutely terrifying!

Retirement can also be seen as a new challenge and growth opportunity. As I previously stated – it all depends on your mindset. With this in mind, perhaps we should look at change differently…

"Change, properly managed, represents an opportunity to fundamentally rethink and redesign our lives for greater control and satisfaction in our retirement."

Change! This is a word that for many of us, we try to avoid. For some, you may even see it as a swear word. We don't want to hear it mentioned, we don't want to apply it, we just don't want anything to do with that word and what it represents. Far too many people try to navigate their life in retirement doing the same old things the same old ways. Whilst this may feel comfortable and it may even feel "right", it will not bring you closer to those goals and dreams you established (or will establish) for your retirement lifestyle plan.

If you don't address the issues and areas that are looming before you as you approach retirement, in the vain hope that they might just go away and disappear all by themselves, you are in for a very uncomfortable surprise! Life just doesn't work that way and, the longer you leave these issues, the fewer options will be open to you to be able to overcome them - so that you can really start to enjoy the retirement phase of your life.

Do not make the rookie mistake of only addressing the "big things". The things that really stand out and are obvious to both yourself and those around you, that need changing, we work at to change (mostly). But it is the little things that, if unchecked and unchallenged, often go from a small issue, to a major problem.

In fact, it's these "little things" that often bring our plans unstuck. Don't dismiss these areas of change in your life - a small change may make a huge impact, over time.

In Chaos theory this is known as "the butterfly effect" which basically proposes that a small change can make much bigger changes happen; that one small incident can have a big impact in the future. (Chaos theory is a mathematical theory that can be used to explain complex systems such as weather, astronomy, politics, and economics. Although many complex systems appear to behave in a random manner, chaos theory shows that, in reality, there is an underlying order – it is just that it is difficult to see).

Why We Resist Change

At a core level we resist change because it makes us uncomfortable. Remember the diagram in section one showing our comfort zone? Well, change is a stimulus that puts us into that "stretch" zone – too much change, over too short a time frame, will put us into the panic zone.

Just how uncomfortable a change will make us feel (and thus how much we are likely to resist it) comes down to two primary reasons: lack of willingness and lack of ability.

- Unwilling – when we are unwilling it is because we either don't understand the longer term benefits or that we are faced with too much change in a short time frame.
- Unable - We fear that we will not be able to learn/adapt to the new situation/environment.

The reasons of resistance towards change can be complex and a detailed explanation is beyond the scope of this book - but here are four to consider

1. Fear of the Unknown

Probably one of the biggest reasons why people resist change. An immediate jump by an individual (or group) to that stretch or panic zone. This is an emotional reaction and is best dealt with through gaining a better understanding of facts (creating a plan – such as your retirement lifestyle plan – is an effective way to gain that better understanding).

2. Comfortable With the Way Things Are

When you are in your comfort zone it is tempting to want to stay there. In retirement, that is a recipe for disaster as, without that stimulus of having to "stretch" every now and then, life becomes tedious and uninteresting.

3. No Perceived Advantage in Doing Something Different

Often benefits of change hide themselves in the medium to long term horizon. It is easy to get a false sense of security by claiming that there is no immediate benefit to the change (in fact, there may be some disadvantages).

4. Lack of Ownership or Involvement in the Change Process

Usually, resistance is passive/aggressive, meaning it is far more underground: people hear you out, saying nothing that is overtly negative, but they do not buy into the necessity for the change(s).

Resistance to change is a natural reaction – that being said, you need to evaluate whether the resistance is warranted (the change really isn't beneficial) or is simply rooted in not wanting to move out of that comfort zone.

How To Manage Change

Where you have identified that the change is required (despite resistance to it) you need to be able to engage a process which allows you to manage the change so that, at the very least, its impacts are not counterproductive to your goals but, more importantly, can be leveraged to your advantage. There are innumerable processes and systems that deal with change management – if you Google the term you will have no shortage of resources to check out.

Two books on the subject that I highly recommend are:

Who Moved My Cheese? by Spencer Johnson and;

Our Iceberg is Melting - by Holger Rathgeber and John Kotter

Here is a five step model to consider when you are looking to manage the changes you need to deal with as you approach and enter retirement:

1. Identify change areas

You are going to have many areas of your life that will need to change as you approach and enter the retirement phase of your life. When you undertake your personal SWOT analysis the opportunities/threats areas are a source of some of the more obvious ones, as is the weaknesses category

2. **Communicate**

   It is important that you also consider those people in your life that will be impacted/involved in these changes and that you include them in the process

3. Develop plans

Apply risk analysis and creative thinking techniques to analyse potential impacts and strategies to deal with these

4. **Action the plans**

   As the change approaches activate the plan. Make sure everyone knows what has to happen and what their role is.

Provide the support and watch out for stress. Maintain some routine as far as is possible. Maintain open communication with all those involved

5. Monitor results

How is the reality v the plan? What is working? What is not? Apply those experiences where practical. Take remedial action as appropriate

Dealing With Resistance To Change In Others

It is not only your own resistance to change that you need to concern yourself with – you also need to be able to identify and manage resistance to change in those around you – especially those that are in your personal inner circle such as your spouse/partner, family members and close personal friends. I will be providing you with some suggestions on how to deal with this in section three's chapter, "The Enemy Without".

Your retirement is looming – maybe it is already upon you – so change is not something to be afraid of. It is, in fact, a key part of your life from this point on. The reality is that it always has been - but it is likely that you have been shielded from many of its direct impacts or have had others to take care of the details up to now. It is your choice as to whether you sit back and just take whatever life throws at you or whether you take advantage of the opportunity that change frequently represents.

Positive change outcomes rely on your ideas, direction, and goals. So be prepared to break out the crayons and paint outside the lines - you might just surprise yourself! Those outcomes also rely on your ability to develop a well-considered plan – and that is what we are going to cover in the next chapter.

There are additional resources on the whole change management issue in the support website (www.whencaniretire.com.au).

A Planning Framework

"Let our advance worrying become advance thinking and planning."
Winston Churchill

I know that I have mentioned this previously, but it's important –
so I'm going to mention it again – your retirement years are a critical
part of your life, it's where you finally get to exercise some real control over how you want to live and, importantly, how you want to be
remembered.

You should not be leaving something as important as this to
chance. Unfortunately, far too many people do. So, to leave as little as
possible to chance you need a plan!

What Is your retirement lifestyle plan meant to do?

Essentially, your retirement lifestyle plan helps you to answer these
4 critical questions:

1.   How do I want to live my life in retirement? – The destination
2.   Where am I right now? – The starting point
3.   How will I get there? – The journey
4.   How will I know if I'm succeeding? – The checkpoints

A good retirement lifestyle plan will address each of these questions and provide clear answers for you, as well as keeping you fo-
cussed and on target - regardless of the distractions that life is going to
throw at you. There are many ways to structure a plan – be it for business or personal. I want to keep things simple for you, in my experience the simpler something is, the more likely we are to actually do it!

I am going to share with you a retirement lifestyle planning process
that contains just five key plan elements and which will help you to
answer the above four questions:

1. Vision

Your vision is your "Why" (we covered that in section one – remember?).

This also assists you in creating your S.M.A.R.T. goals – these are the "milestones" that mark your progress against how you want to live your life in retirement. This answers the question as to your destination.

2. Situation

Here's where you assess your current state. Remember those tools I shared with you earlier (SWOT/PESTEL)? Here's where you'll be using them. This answers the "where am I now?" question

3. Strategy

If you understand where you are now and where you want to be, you need to document how you intend to bridge that gap. For each of your goals how do you envision yourself reaching them?

Here you are also going to need to establish what resources will be required as well as what actions need to be taken. This answers the "how will I get there?" question

4. Accountability

This is such a small detail, but it is also one of the key elements of a retirement lifestyle plan that so many people fail to consider. There are going to be many things in your retirement plan that you, ultimately, are responsible for. However, that does not mean that you have to do everything in the plan yourself.

When you are not performing a particular action, who is? And to what extent should you hold them accountable?

A lack of accountability will absolutely destroy your strategy execution. Lacking or confusing accountability results in:

- Outcomes not being delivered because no-one knew who was responsible for what
- Conflicting interpretations of what needs to happen next
- Finger pointing and blame shifting when things don't go to plan

This supports the question, "how will I get there?"

5. KPIs (Key Performance Indicators)

Creating KPIs is one of the hardest of all the key elements of your retirement plan. But without KPIs, you won't know, until it's too late, as to whether or not you're succeeding as you head towards your vision. Your KPIs should relate to how well you're going against the components of your strategies.

Don't let setting KPIs become harder than it needs to be – and you don't need more than one or two KPIs for each of your goals. But you do need to ensure that your KPIs accurately reflect what success actually looks like for that goal, and also that you'll be able to accurately measure the KPI on a regular basis. Selecting the right KPIs is, therefore, one of the key elements of an effective retirement lifestyle plan. This answers the question "how will I know if I'm succeeding?"

There's a tool that will assist you with formulating your KPI's in the resources area of the website. (www.whencaniretire.com.au).

As you are working on your retirement plan you will find that you need to go back and forth to add/remove elements as the plan is developed. Completing the plan is an iterative process not a linear one.

You may even find that you need to revisit some of your goals – especially when you calculate what it might cost to achieve them (either in time, money or other resources).

That's fine – in fact, it happens often. The best time to be adding, deleting and amending details is in the planning stages – it's one of the reasons that formal planning (such as I am outlining here) is such a powerful tool. Because making changes in the planning stages is far less costly and disruptive than making changes once you enter your retirement!

The Devil Is In The Details

"Thinking is easy, acting is difficult, and to put one's thoughts into action is the most difficult thing in the world."
Johann Wolfgang von Goethe

By this stage of the plan development process your retirement lifestyle plan is really starting to take shape – the one thing that is missing though are the action steps needed to enable the plan to be activated and move you towards your goals.

All the planning in the world will not deliver success for you unless your plan translates into action. You achieve this by revisiting your goals – for each goal you will need to list all of those things that need to be completed for the goal to be achieved. These are your action items. Make sure that you list everything that needs to be done to achieve the goal– not just those things that you, personally, will be doing. You will also need to estimate how long each item is likely to take to complete, as this will provide you with information as to whether your time frame for the goal is realistic. At this point you should also start to think about the money/resources that will be required to complete the actions required to complete the goal.

Once you have completed your action items you need to establish an order for them (more on this later). Some of your goals will be more important to you than others – these should become your priority goals and the action items associated with their completion should always take precedence over lower priority goal action items.

There are five very important reasons for establishing these priorities:

1. To obtain key pay offs from completing high priority actions first
2. To ensure specifically identified needs are met first.
3. Acting according to the chosen priorities, builds commitment in yourself and others.
4. Prioritising increases your credibility.
5. Prioritising helps deal with procrastination

Next Action Decision Making

I strongly recommend that you only prioritise your goals – not the action steps associated with them, as all you end up with when you prioritize action steps is list after list of "priorities" which, with the dynamic and changing world we live in, renders them useless in quick time!

Instead, I suggest that you adopt the principle of "next actions" – what is the next thing that needs to be done in order to move you closer to that goal's completion?

This process results in:

- Better focus on the here and now
- Takes moments to decide
- Minimises procrastination
- Reduces pressure
- Aids decision making
- Fosters accountability (who should be doing this?)
- Increases your ability to make things happen

Here's how you do that….

Create a page for each goal you have established for your retirement plan and list, in order, the "next actions" required for that goal to be achieved.

You should be able to fit all of this on the equivalent of a single A4 sheet of paper for each goal. If you can't, you need to break the goal down into a set of minor goals with each of these having their own single sheet.

I have found that single goals with multiple pages of action steps are too complex – it becomes confusing and, as a result, the goal often gets put into the "too hard" basket

I introduced "next action" decision making in Section one of the book, it was in the chapter "What's Your Passion". Here's the process for you again:

To establish your "next Steps" for each goal is fairly straight forward;

1. Pick one of your goals
2. Ask yourself, "what would be the last thing I would need to have happen for this goal to be completed?" Record this as your last step
3. Then ask yourself, "what would need to happen immediately before that (last step)?" Record this as your second last step.
4. Repeat the process until you can answer the question, "what would need to be the first thing to have to happen, to start towards completing this goal?"

I call this my "next Steps" sheet. There's a template for this on the support website (www.whencaniretire.com.au).

Once you have completed this process, for each of your goals, you have a set of "next Steps" which are going to be your action items. This provides you with the order of what needs to happen.

This process will provide you with a very flexible action step plan that is not reliant on day to day or week to week priority lists that only end up changing all the time due to elements, mostly outside of your control (and unforeseen), which change your immediate, and sometimes long term, plans.

With this system, when the unexpected happens, you can pause your action steps, deal with the unexpected situation and then resume where you left off. You do not have to regenerate a new priorities list each time something out of the blue comes along! We all know that life is like that – remember "Murphy's Law"?

I will show you an example of this as I run through the scheduling process with you.

Scheduling Next Steps

Now you have your goals, along with the action steps that need to be taken in order to reach them. You have a clear picture as to **what** has to happen and in what order.

Now what you have to do is start thinking about a schedule – this will give you a clearer picture as to **when** things need to happen.

This is when things start to get a little more complicated, as you attempt to fit everything into your schedule – you have multiple goals, each with their own action steps. As you start to meld these together in a single schedule, it is highly likely that you will realise that you can't fit everything in. Especially when you consider your current responsibilities – you are probably not retired yet, so you have a lot of other pressures to deal with and tasks to perform. Even if you are semi or recently retired, you are going to have other responsibilities that you are dealing with and need to make allowances for. This is normal and is all a part of the process (hey! That's life, isn't it?) – so don't panic or start to doubt that your plan will work. It will - you just may need to revisit some of your goals and timelines.

You have established your high priority goals and your action steps process shows you what you need to be doing and in what order Your problem is that you have a LOT of things that have to be completed within a defined time frame and you get STUCK because you don't know how to fit it all in. Begin by accepting that you probably won't do everything "In order of priority" any'more. I can't remember the last day I did everything "in order."

In other words, you have your "next steps" list for each goal and you have your schedule (I'll come here shortly) and you have your daily plan laid out for today/tomorrow. Most days it's not going to happen in the precise sequence you laid it out.

Example: Today I'm writing content for this book, which means I switch between researching that content and writing it. I am not looking at my email inbox and my telephone calls are going to voice mail

IF SEVENTY IS THE NEW FIFTY• 179

(I have to do this or the distractions that these represent prevent me from hitting my daily word count target for the book).

Later today I will be working on a couple of client projects – I do all of my writing for the book in the morning.

On a break (yes, you need those!), I get up to make myself a cuppa (Green tea with fresh ginger, in case you're wondering) and, whilst I am waiting for the kettle to boil, I check my phone messages - in case there's anything urgent I need to deal with. I don't check emails during my writing time, as a delay in responding to an email is rarely mission critical (unless in your job or your business you use email for mission critical matters – which I do not).

There's one message (out of four) that is urgent. So, my break is postponed whilst I deal with that message. It takes me just under an hour to resolve my client's problem – I now have a very happy client but have lost a big chunk of time that I wasn't expecting to lose.

No drama – I just removed from today's schedule a non-critical next step from one of my other project goals that I had expected to take around an hour and rescheduled it. I did not have to reassess my priorities and create a whole new list. If you don't work this way, I'm betting that you procrastinate (more on this soon) – quite a bit. At times, this leads to a "brain freeze" that results in doing nothing of value for longer and longer periods of time.

With a well-thought out schedule that is based on this "next step" actions process you minimise procrastination.

Back to that schedule . Okay, so you have a schedule that is, currently, overcrowded. Here's what you do:

1. Identify the actions associated with your high priority goals
2. Remove any actions that are not associated with high priority goals
3. Re-evaluate the schedule
4. If the schedule now permits it, start adding action items for the lower priority goals until you are comfortable that the schedule is workable

5. If the schedule is still too crowded remove some of your higher priority goal "next actions" until the schedule seems workable

6. Add the items you removed from that schedule to a later schedule

This process means that you need to reassess the timelines for your lower priority goals until you reach that "sweet spot" where your time horizon allows the schedule to work. Do not overcommit yourself with a packed schedule – you are simply begging for trouble and a plan that will not deliver on your vision. Again, after delivering hundreds of workshops in the corporate arena on productivity and time management, I can attest to the fact that most people think they have more time over which they exercise control than they actually do. This results in establishing unrealistic schedules. Let's face it, if you think that you have nine hours in a day which you have control over, you are going to schedule nine hours' worth of action steps.

What happens if, in reality, you only have six hours that you can control? You end up with an impossible schedule (even though it looked fine to begin with) which, in turn, puts you under increased pressure, resulting in stress and burnout as you try frantically to catch up – day, after day, after day!

Here is the bad news – on any given day, you have far less control of your time than you think. Unexpected telephone calls, family members, friends, employees, colleagues – the list goes on (and on) – all take time away from what you thought you control. In reality, if you can control forty percent of your time you are doing well. So, when establishing your schedule, you have to take this into account - otherwise your plan will not materialise, and you will forever be wondering why.

I would also recommend that you break your master schedule down into a series of short time frame windows. Your master schedule represents all of the action steps required to achieve your goals – as a result it is likely to be quite long and will not provide you with focus.

The master schedule's purpose is to establish whether your goal time-lines are realistic.

Once you have established that, it is time to break down that schedule into a series of shorter term schedules so as to provide you with focus. Here's what developing that would look like. I have used a ninety day timeframe, but you can select whatever timeframe works for you.

90 Day Schedule

1. Create a 90 Day Focus

Your master schedule will be overwhelming in its scope. Develop a time period that inspires action by reducing/eliminating that overwhelm.

- Keep it simple.
- Identify Key Performance Indicators (KPI's – explained in the next chapter)
- Nominate which goals are being addressed (depending on your selected timeframe some of your goals may not feature in a broken down schedule)

2. Build in Accountability

You may not, personally, be completing every action step. Where this is the case it is important to ensure that such tasks have assigned owners and deadlines.

3. Create Checkpoints

Communication is critical to keeping on track.

- Regularly review progress (you decide an appropriate frequency for this).
- If any action step is delayed determine why.
- Identify barriers
- Look for solutions to any potential issues.

4. Review & Create Your Next 90 Day Focus

Ensure before starting on the next schedule that you review your 90 day focus with regards to what was achieved and what wasn't;

- Did you hit objectives as a result of the action steps carried out?

- What did you learn that can be applied to the next 90 days?
- Revisit you master schedule
- With the previous 90 days and your master schedule in mind, set your next 90 day focus and go through the process again

It isn't complicated but it does require work. I have found that by keeping the scheduling process simple you can maintain a focus on achievement. It also means that you do not have to be reviewing your whole plan all the time - you are either on track or not. If you are on track keep going, if not, review the plan to see if anything needs to be adjusted in light of your experience.

Procrastination

Procrastination is an all too common issue. Whether you're having trouble getting started, getting finished or you're stuck somewhere in between, it's very frustrating indeed.

Why do we procrastinate? What is it that holds you back? As with any issue you might have, you need to look carefully at the feelings that arise when thinking about the issue. Are you afraid that you might fail, or perhaps even afraid that you might succeed? Are you feeling de-motivated by it or bored at the prospect of having to do it? Is it the 'wrong' time? Do you feel you aren't able to do the job; lacking enough experience or information to do it properly?

Overwhelm is often at the heart of our procrastination – there is so much to be done that we simply don't know where to start, so we don't! Putting your retirement lifestyle plan together is a case in point – planning is both time consuming and complex, even though the principles of planning are simple.

What to do about it?

First, identify your whys and do something with them, it's all about making sure you have the right mindset and approach. Examine the planning process I have outlined in this section of the book and see if you can identify the source of your reluctance – have you lost sight of your purpose, don't have an outcome clearly defined, too few options/ideas (or too many), neglected to organise your options or to assign next actions?

Here are some other suggestions:

- Take a first step forward. Sometimes, we feel we've bitten off more than we can chew. And one of the most effective ways to get over that feeling is to do something (anything really!) just to get things going. Choose something that you know you can achieve, and do it, congratulate yourself and then move on to the next task.
- Know your goals and motivation Often we put things off because we don't have a clear 'vision' of what we want our final outcome to be. When your goal is fuzzy, this impacts your energy levels, your motivation and naturally your output. You need to be very clear about what it is you want to achieve and how this will benefit you. Once you have established a positive base, you then have more leverage to incite yourself into action. If you know how something is going to be of benefit to you, you're more likely to do it.
- Plan your deadlines We all need deadlines! If you don't have a specific end point in mind, you're far less likely to achieve it. So be very clear on when a particular task needs to be done by, and then work backwards from that date, identifying smaller steps leading ultimately to the main goal.
- Focus on what's important (rather than urgent) Rather than being side-tracked by lots of perceived "urgent" issues, remember that it is the important tasks which get you closer to your goal.
- Listen to yourself Each of us has a unique body clock and concentration curve. By matching your task to the

right time of day, and how you are feeling, you can have a big impact on your effectiveness. Choose to deal with the most demanding tasks when your natural energy is at its highest, and you will get more done in less time.

- Acknowledge your achievements Very importantly too, after achieving each major step towards your goal, take time to acknowledge yourself, congratulate yourself, for having done so. You would do that for a good friend or colleague, so why not do it for yourself?

Success Indicators

"The safest road to hell is the gradual one - the gentle slope, soft underfoot, without sudden turnings, without milestones, without signposts."
C. S. Lewis

You have a retirement lifestyle plan – congratulations! You have a realistic schedule for all of your action steps – well done! The question now is, how will you know if you are on track to achieve your goals?

By now you will be realising that your retirement lifestyle plan document is going to be quite lengthy – so you don't want to have to read through the entire thing just to check if you are still on track. By all means, review your plan's contents regularly but, if you just want to check the "pulse" of your progress the best and quickest way to do that is by understanding what your success indicators are.

You come to that understanding through establishing some Key Performance Indicators (KPI's)

KPI's are used in the business world, by well managed businesses, to provide a mechanism whereby the health or pulse of the business can be quickly assessed – in terms of how well the business is performing compared to its business or strategic plan.

What exactly is a KPI?

In simple terms, a KPI is a way of measuring how well we, as individuals (or how well entire companies or business units), are performing. They are a measurable value that demonstrates how effectively you are progressing towards your retirement plan goals.

Good KPIs:

- Provide objective evidence of progress towards achieving your desired result.
- Measure what is intended to be measured to help inform better decision making.
- Offer a comparison that gauges the degree of performance change over time.

The metrics that you measure, and track depend completely on your retirement lifestyle plan goals. Metrics are measures of quantitative assessment which you will use for assessing, comparing, and tracking your results and progress.

Here's a simple process to assist you in establishing your KPI metrics:

1. Select one of your goals.
2. Next, consider how you can measure the progress towards that goal.
3. Your KPI will be the achievement of one of the key action steps which indicates that you are on track to achieve the goal.

KEY POINT:

Only establish the KPIs that are relevant and mission critical to YOUR goals. This is not about measuring everything associated with a goal – only those critical things that, if achieved, indicate that things are on track.

In other words, you are only going to measure the big stuff because, all things being equal, the little stuff tends to take care of itself if the big stuff is okay.

You'll probably only need 2 or 3 KPIs per goal (1 ea for beginning stage, middle and end of goal progress status).

Here are some examples of the KPI's that Iris and I established when we put our plan together:

- Australian Citizenship for Dennis

I needed to secure Australian Citizenship because my residency visa was subject to my not being out of the country for more than two years.

There was quite a bit involved in this but the KPI's we established were;

- o Citizenship test booked
- o Citizenship ceremony date confirmed
- o Passport application submitted

We felt that, if the above were completed the minor details would all be slotting into place.

- • Moving clients online (Dennis)

My client base was predominantly built on face to face contact – especially for delivery of corporate training workshops and executive coaching.

- o Potential digital clients identified
- o Non digital clients hand overs completed
- o Digital clients activated

Again, there was a lot more activity involved in making this happen but the above three KPI's were an excellent "pulse" to check.

- • Secure employment (Iris)

Iris intended to secure a teaching job at an International school in Germany. For the previous 10 years she had been in a senior admin role. There was a lot she needed to do to transition and secure employment.

- o Resume updated
- o International teacher membership activated
- o Approach emails sent to target schools
- o Three interviews secured

The above KPI's provided us with a check against critical tasks – if these were successfully completed, the rest would fall into place. That is what a KPI is all about!

- • Pre-departure (Dennis and Iris)

We had a set number of action steps across multiple goals (including the KPI's in the above three examples). Rather than continually checking all we simply totalled up all the action steps and then measure how many ticks we had at each of the below points in time.

- o   18 months out: 10% of key actions completed
- o   12 months out: 25% of key actions completed
- o   6 months out: 40% of key actions completed
- o   3 months out: 60% of key actions completed
- o   1 month out: 75% of key actions completed

If we found ourselves not hitting a particular KPI we could then dig deeper to see where the issue was and what to do about it. As our plan incorporated our first three months after arrival it was not going to be 100% completed until after arrival – so we continued the KPI monitoring when that happened.

- •   Arrival
- o   1 month in: 90% of key actions completed
- o   3 months in: 100% of key actions completed

We did not achieve 100% at three months after arrival. However, the tasks we did not complete were, largely, inconsequential. By establishing our KPI's we were able to monitor our progress and identify any roadblocks before they became critical issues.

Did everything go according to plan? Definitely not! However, having the plan (complete with contingency actions in case of something not working out) and the KPI's as a monitoring tool, allowed us to undertake a significant life event without stressing ourselves out.

Knowing What You Don't Know

"He who is not every day conquering some fear has not learned the secret of life."
Ralph Waldo Emmerson

If the penny hasn't dropped for you already, it's about to… Along your journey in life you never stop learning – some lessons we welcome and actively seek out. Others are thrust upon us whether we like it or not! As you begin taking steps to take more control over your life, so that you can enjoy your longevity bonus to its fullest, you are going to have to learn some new skills and be prepared to apply them rigorously.

We have already covered some ground in this space and I am not about to repeat myself here – well, not to any great extent anyhow – after all, for each person reading this book, that term "new skills" will refer to a whole different spectrum of skills – what is new to one person is going to be old hat to someone with a different career path and life experience. Which "new skills" are going to be most important to you?

As far as the contents of this book are concerned it is most probably those concepts and processes that you are, presently, most resistant to. You know the ones – you don't (yet) see their relevance to you or you have discounted their validity in your circumstances, or you have simply labelled them as "too difficult".

This is a prime example of a dark inner force of "resistance" and self-sabotage at work – a concept we will be looking at in the next section of the book in the chapter "The Enemy Within". When you decide to establish a "side hustle" or business based upon what it is that you love, there are inherent skills and knowledge you will need which will enhance your ability to both launch, grow and sustain that business.

Here are a few of the key knowledge and skill areas to consider:

Technology

Us older folk do not have a great reputation when it comes to our understanding of technology. In fact, the younger generations often deride us over it and consider us to be something akin to Luddites!

In many cases this is very true but in others, not so much. Wherever you sit on that continuum one thing is for sure – you have to be able to make technology your new best friend. The reason is obvious but I'm going to state it anyhow – technology is the platform upon which so many business models are now based. In fact, technology has woven itself so intricately into the fabric of life that we often do not realise when we are benefiting from it.

Consider these:

- ATM's - I don't know about you but I remember the days when you had to make sure that you had enough cash to tide you over the weekend because if you ran out there were no ATM's for you to get more (and credit cards were not in common use) so, unless you had a friendly business that would cash a cheque for you, life got very interesting!
- Internet – this has changed the world! It is the base for so many of our daily activities – social media, email, online shopping (and banking) are just a few of dozens (perhaps hundreds) of examples.
- GPS – I, like you, remember the frustration of trying to navigate using printed street directories!
- Smartphones -not just a phone in your pocket (which is amazing enough on its own) but also a camera, internet browser, calculator, GPS, diary, weather bureau and so much more

The list is almost endless and I'm sure I don't need to add to the above to demonstrate the point that technology is an essential part of life in the 21st Century. You simply cannot afford to dismiss it or pig-headedly try to ignore the need for you to get a handle on the technology that can make a difference in your life – and for the side hustle or business you are considering supporting your longevity bonus going forward. That is not to say, though, that you need to fully understand all of the technology that society has embraced – only those technologies that are relevant for your needs.

Even then, you do not need to have a deep understanding of how the technology works -you only need understand how to drive it for your needs.

It's like a motor vehicle, most people need a car in today's world, but you only need to know how to drive it and what the driving regulations are. You don't need to understand how a car works nor have the expertise to repair and service it. It's the same with technology, decide what technologies you need and to what extent you need to learn to apply and use them and then begin your learning journey from there - I'll be exploring that process with you very shortly.

If technology intimidates you, that learning journey will be more difficult to start upon but, like anything else in life, you have to start somewhere. Putting it off (and off and off!) is not going to get you to where you need to be. Bite the bullet or, as Brian Tracy would say, "Eat that frog!". Before you know it, you will be engaging and leveraging technology in ways you never thought possible!

Negotiation Skills

Here's a skill that is so critical but yet so misunderstood by so many. In life you do net get what you deserve – only what you can negotiate for. Since the late 1990's I have delivered negotiation skills courses to tens of thousands of people in Australia and around the world and the most common misconception I experience is that people do not realise just how often they negotiate. I'm willing to bet that you don't either – and here's why: You are in negotiation situations so often you simply do not recognise the opportunity when it is staring you in the face! Here are some typical situations where negotiation situations arise but you are blissfully unaware that they're happening:

- You and your partner (spouse, significant other, etc) have decided to have an evening out. You want to go out for a meal, they want to go out and see a show. You start having a conversation around that. This is a negotiation, but most people don't see it that way.

- Your teenage child wants to go out with their friends and wants to stay out until 11pm. You want them home by 10pm. You start having a conversation around that. This is a negotiation, but most people don't see it that way

- Your work colleague needs your assistance with a project. You want to assist but can't do so in the time frame they are requesting. You start having a discussion around that. This is a negotiation, but most people don't see it that way

- Your boss wants you to work some overtime over the next two weeks, but you have family commitments that limit your availability for the next three weeks. You start to discuss options with each other. This is a negotiation, but most people don't see it that way

These are but a few of the sorts of negotiation opportunities people find themselves in without realising that they are negotiating and that is why we often end up with soured relationships or feeling hard done by as a result of a conversation not going the way we would have liked. If you have ever come away from a conversation with someone and regretted the decisions or commitments you made as a result (of that conversation), chances are you missed recognising the negotiation opportunity that was before you. Negotiations happen all the time – how often you ask?

Well, the opportunity to negotiate exists anytime that two or more people are seeking to influence the other's thinking or actions. As you can't influence a negotiation outcome unless you are aware you are in a negotiating situation, the first step in becoming a better negotiator is to recognise that opportunity. Your next step is then to upgrade your knowledge around the principles of negotiation. I am not going to go into that here as it would be another book in itself, however I have put together a negation skills primer for you which you can access in the resources section of the support website. (www.whencanire-tire.com.au).

Selling skills

Here's another skill that we all use without realising it. The term "selling skills" is often applied to those fast talking, high pressure people who are not letting you out of their sights until you have bought something from them. We have all experienced this at some point but, in reality, it is not really what selling is all about. Selling is another word for influencing and it is what each and every one of us do, at various times, during our week, in our interactions with others.

We are trying to influence people almost every time we engage with them – not just in business but also in our day to day lives – so it makes absolute sense to improve and master our influencing skills. Here are a couple of examples of selling skills in action in day to day life:

- You have decided to move suburbs, which will mean a change in school for your children. They are not too keen on the idea so you sit down with them and emphasize all the great things that will happen as a result of the move (you may even incorporate a few incentives or bribes for them as a part of the talk). In the end your children get on board with the idea. You have just used selling skills in influencing your children's thinking about the move.

- There is a concert that you want to go to but you do not want to go alone. You have a friend who may be interested but who hasn't thought about going along. You have a conversation with that friend which starts from a position where they initially resist the idea but eventually agree. Moving someone from "no" to "maybe" and eventually, "yes" is a demonstration of selling skills

Selling skills involve influencing a person to take on board a position they may not have otherwise welcomed or thought much about. Negotiation skills involve agreeing on any terms associated with them taking that position on. Whatever side hustle or business idea you want to give birth to, you are going to need to engage in conversations designed to influence the thinking and positions of others – that is selling skills and you need to master the skill as much as possible. Again, like with negotiation skills, I am not going to go into detail here on how to improve your selling skills as that's another entire book. So here, again, is a link to the support website resource that will at least start you on that journey: www.whencaniretire.com.au

Communication Skills

Communication is another critical life skill and, before you start thinking that you are already pretty good at it I'm betting that you could be a lot better – and you will need to be when it comes to making your side hustle work for you (as opposed to you working for it!).

Communication can be broken down into two main components:

1. Sending a message (talking, writing as examples)
2. Receiving a message (listening, reading as examples)

There are more but, for the sake of expediency, we will concentrate on these two

Sending a Message

There are several ways you can send a message; this is referred to as the "medium". Mediums include; face to face, telephone, video, email, etc. Choice of the right medium is crucial in ensuring that your message is understood.

You may need to modify your message – either in terms of its content, structure or detail, depending on the medium. For example; if you were communicating over the phone you may need to be prepared to add more detail to your content as you do not have the benefit of seeing each other's facial expression or body language.

With face to face conversations you need to be conscious of your body language (it must support your message), as well as your tone of voice as both of these elements can substantially alter the perceived meaning of the message(s) sent. Just try delivering bad news, in person, to another person whilst you maintain a smile on your face – the other person will struggle to take the message seriously.

With written communication your grammar and punctuation are critical if your message is to be understood as you mean it. As an example, here is a straightforward sentence:

"A woman without her man is useless!"

Now, read it again with different punctuation:
"A woman, without her, man is useless!"

Most of us do not give our communication a second thought because we are doing it so often, but it is dangerous to assume that people understand what we are saying – otherwise miscommunication happens and that can be disastrous!

Receiving a Message

We can receive a message through visual mediums (as in video), listening (as with face to face and telephone) or through reading (as with email and printed matter). By far, the area where most of us need significant improvement is with listening – we do a poor job of listening to others and the best example of that is when we are introduced to someone for the first time.

How often have you been introduced to someone and within a minute you have forgotten their name? It's not that you didn't hear them properly, you just weren't paying close enough attention to them when they gave their name to you.

You need to improve your communication skills in order to be better understood, as well as to be able to understand others better and just as with negotiation skills and communication skills it would take a whole other book for me to run through with you how to do this. The support website has a communications and listening skills primer that you may find useful. (www.whencaniretire.com.au).

Your Learning Journey

As adults, whenever we embark on a learning journey – whether it is forced upon us by circumstance or whether we take it on voluntarily – we go through the same stages. These stages are referred to as the "Competency Model" of learning and are illustrated in figure eight.

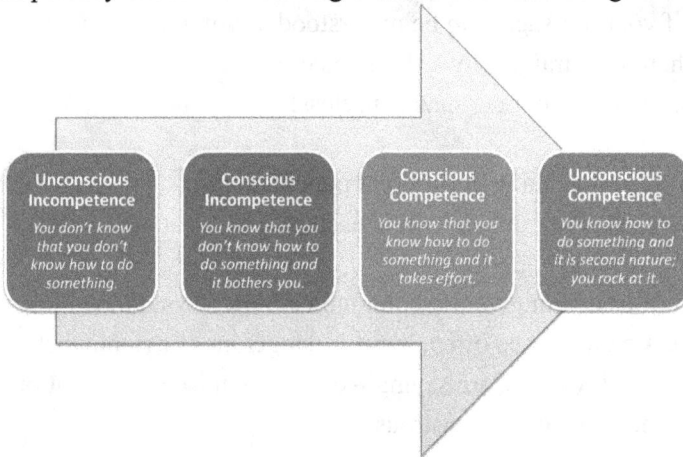

Figure 8: Competency Learning Model

As an example, let's take a situation that the vast majority of people will have experienced - that of learning to drive a motor vehicle.

Unconscious Incompetence

Your experience of travelling in a car is as a passenger. You do not take much notice of what's involved and, even when you do (as you approach an age where driving a car becomes a possibility) it looks reasonably straightforward.

Conscious Incompetence

You have your first driving lesson and what an eye opener it is! Many things to do and remember! You doubt that you will ever be able to do it successfully.

Conscious Competence

IF SEVENTY IS THE NEW FIFTY• 197

After much practise (and plenty of mistakes along the way!) you start to develop an understanding of the requirements and you actually become good enough at driving to pass a driving test. However, it still takes a lot of concentration to do so safely.

Unconscious Competence

You have been driving for some time and have become very skilled – so much so that you do not have to focus too much on the driving process and find yourself able to drive for long stretches at a time with little fatigue, even being able to have conversations with others whilst driving!

This is a universal model. Knowing about it helps you to better understand why you react the way you do along your learning journey. Armed with that knowledge you can better strategize your learning approach to be able to develop your skills to the level they need to be in order that you can achieve what you may have thought previously was not possible for you.

Section Two Summary

This section of the book has been all about establishing your retirement lifestyle plan and I'm betting that, if you haven't had much experience around formal, structured planning, you will have been a little surprised at how much is involved in this process.

You will never be truly successful by just taking each day as it comes – you need a plan. This is especially the case as you approach and consider retirement and the sort of lifestyle you want to be able to create for yourself.

I am hoping that you have read through this section of the book in its entirety before starting on your retirement lifestyle plan. Then, having digested those contents, you are soon going to start to put your own retirement lifestyle plan together. Remember that the structure of a book requires information to be presented in a linear form, so page twelve follows page eleven, which follows page ten and so on. You are going to find that developing your retirement lifestyle plan will not exactly follow that structure.

Here's a snapshot of what was covered in this section:
WALK BEFORE YOU RUN
- Don't allow yourself to get caught up in the excitement of your retirement future. Take small, measured, steps
- Apply Demming's Plan/Do/Act/Check process
- Always start with the end (destination) in mind

KNOWING WHERE YOU WANT TO BE
- The three core elements of any journey – Destination/Start Point/Method (for getting there)

- How to create SMART goals
- Prioritising your goals

KNOW WHERE YOU ARE
- Do not allow yourself to fall into the trap of believing you are further ahead than you are
- Conducting a personal audit – it has to be accurate and detailed
- SWOT analysis
- PESTEL analysis

DISCOVERING YOUR WHY
- Your why fuels your passion which provides you with energy
- Energy is what you will need to keep going in the face of obstacles
- Be proactive – in retirement it's all down to you
- Sion Sinek and why
- Questions to ask yourself to identify your why

DEALING WITH OBSTACLES
- No plan survives intact when introduced to the real world
- Preparing yourself for bumps in the road
- Three types of obstacles – Personal/Social/Environmental
- Don't forget Murphy's Law and remember that he was an optimist
- How to overcome obstacles
- Obstacles are not the problem but your reaction to them can be

THINKING CREATIVELY
- Don't react (to obstacles) – respond
- Using creative thinking to identify potential solutions
- Using analytical thinking to establish the suitability of potential solutions
- Barriers to creative thinking

- Identifying obstacles and potential solutions

CHANGE AND WHY RESISTANCE IS FUTILE
- Change is all around us all of the time
- Retirement is about change
- Look at change differently – as an opportunity
- Why we resist change
- Manage change or it will manage you
- The five step change management model
- Dealing with resistance to change in others

A PLANNING FRAMEWORK
- Your retirement plan needs to answer four questions

1. How do I want to live my life in retirement?
2. Where am I right now?
3. How will I get to where I want to be?
4. How will I know if I am succeeding?

- Your retirement plan structure and process

THE DEVIL IS IN THE DETAILS
- Your plan will not work, no matter how detailed it is, unless it translates into action
- Prioritising you goals
- Establishing your action steps using the "Next steps" process
- Creating a master schedule and breaking this down to shorter term time horizons (eg; 90 days)
- Understanding how much of your time you actually control
- Identifying and dealing with procrastination

SUCCESS INDICATORS
- You have to be able to quickly and easily monitor your progress
- Tracking and measuring everything takes too much tie and effort
- Key Performance Indicators (KPI's) – the critical results around which everything else depends

KNOWING WHAT YOU DON'T KNOW

- You need to make technology your friend because everything relies on it in the 21st Century
- Negotiation skills are essential for life in general and business in particular and you negotiate far more than you think
- You don't need to be a super salesperson but you do need to understand that selling is really more about influence than force or clever scripts
- Communication skills – especially listening – are going to be a huge help for you in whatever you do
- There's a process we all go through when learning new skills. Being aware of that process and recognising it in yourself will speed up your learning journey.

If you haven't downloaded and utilised the companion workbook as you progressed through section two, I would suggest that, before you head to section three of the book, you at least sketch out your retirement lifestyle plan, as this will not only reinforce what you have just learned but also show you how many gaps you have in terms of required information to make your plan complete.

The next section of the book is all about translating all of the hard work you have put into the planning process into action.

Engaging The Plan

As you start to read this section of the book you should, at least, have completed a draft or sketch version of your retirement lifestyle plan completed. The gaps in this will show you where you have more work to do – both in terms of research and forward thinking. By having this draft at hand, you will find it easier to apply some of the concepts and suggestions I have for you in this section of the book.

If that's not the way you work, and you are reading the whole of the book before starting on your retirement lifestyle plan, that's fine too – you can still do that and end up where you need to be. It's just that having a draft plan by your side at this point will definitely help you to understand where all of the upcoming content fits for you.

Your retirement lifestyle plan document is going to be substantial – it has to be if you are going to cover everything that you need to. Notwithstanding that, no matter how comprehensive it is, it is not going to make any difference to your life unless you can translate your plan into action! That is what this section of the book is all about.

You will need to have the right mindset to launch your plan and, once launched, you are going to have to be able to remain focused. Your plan is going to cover a lengthy time span, so be prepared to celebrate your wins along the way as a mechanism to keep your levels of motivation high. You are also going to need to deal with the enemy within – which usually manifests itself as procrastination, as well as dealing with resistance in those around you – yes, even those who love you!

You are also going to need to consider what your trigger points – circumstances which invoke a rethink of your retirement lifestyle plan or a particular objective - might look like and what you will do if they eventuate. All of this, and more, is going to be covered over the next set of pages – so, let's keep moving!

Ready Set Go

"Take time to deliberate, but when the time for action has arrived, stop thinking and go in."
Napoleon Bonaparte

For the last five years I have been a Business Development Coach and Digital Marketer. Basically, I work with people to help them grow their businesses and improve their bottom line. This invariably involves a good deal of time spent with them to develop a plan which they can implement for themselves. Whilst there is a lot of work involved in this (much the same as you have a lot of work ahead of you to develop your retirement lifestyle plan), it is also exciting.

Once a business owner or CEO starts to see the potential that the plan, I assist them to develop for themselves represents, their excitement is palpable – they really can't wait for things to start to happen once they launch the plan. However, invariably, there comes a moment—usually as plan launch day gets nearer - when I can sense a bit of turmoil brewing. It sometimes manifests as project delays like;

"I know I need to get stuff to you, I'm so sorry! I've just been insanely busy!"

Other times it's more direct and comes up in conversation,

"This is so overwhelming, I'm nervous as hell! You can be honest, what do you really think about what we're planning?"

At times I feel more like a therapist than a Business Development Coach! Being a business owner myself for over 20 years, I know exactly what they're going through. Here's a really important lesson to take away from these experiences - your mindset can actually be the most powerful factor in making your retirement lifestyle plan a success.

Here's the thing when it comes to being successful (in just about every situation) … If you don't believe in yourself and your plan, the best strategies in the world are still going to fall short.

When you enter retirement the buck really does start and stop with you - you are your most important resource. You are your biggest advocate and cheerleader. Which is why a positive mindset and belief in yourself is essential to making your retirement lifestyle plan successful. Mastering your mindset is key if you want to be able to enjoy this "Longevity bonus" that retirement represents in the twenty first century.

I don't mean this to sound harsh, but if you don't believe in yourself, why would anyone else believe in you? On the flip side, if you have confidence, it will shine through in everything that you do. This does not mean that you will eliminate your doubts and areas of uncertainty – you will always have those. Despite these, having the right mindset prevents you from succumbing to the base fears that these doubts raise within you.

This is another benefit of having a well-structured and thought out retirement lifestyle plan. Whenever your inner demons surface and try to convince you that you are not going to succeed, your plan is a reminder as to why these fears, whilst natural, are unfounded. Make no mistake, activating your plan and embarking on your retirement journey will, at times, be a daunting prospect and there will be many moments throughout the process that will make you question yourself. That's normal and with experience you'll find your confidence will increase and mindset will become more positive.

Before you decide to flick the switch and activate your retirement lifestyle plan, makes sure that you have first of all engaged a winning mindset. I want to help you shift your mindset NOW – so you can experience great results with your plan.

When you find yourself in need of a confidence boost here are five ways you can get into a more confident mindset:

1. Revisit Success

Everyone approaching retirement has a lifetime of experience behind them. So, focus on some positives from that experience bank you have. Think about some past successes – times when you really nailed it! Think about how that made you feel and start to recreate those feelings in the here and now. Make a list of 4-6 of these and keep referring to them. This is "social proof" of your ability to be successful. If you did it before, you can do it again.

2. Practice Self-Care

An important part of cultivating a healthy and positive mindset is practicing self-care. It is very easy to slip into a pattern where you aren't taking time for your mental and physical health. That takes its toll on you. I recently realised that I hadn't been getting exercise on a regular basis. While I know it's important, I had so many reasons (make that excuses) for why I wasn't making time for it. When I added in morning walks, I discovered that my mindset improved dramatically.

3. Trust Yourself

Self-doubt has to be the number one threat to a positive mindset. Whilst it is a perfectly natural reaction to those times when you are going to attempt something new, you cannot allow it to get in the way of moving forward. When you allow self-doubt to fester it leads to anxiety and "worst case scenario" thinking. Don't think too far into the future and letting your brain swim around and around in circles. Stay present and trust yourself that whatever it is you can figure it out or fix it.

Your retirement lifestyle plan will not prepare you for every contingency. There are going to be challenges, and you can't predict and plan for all of them. Your plan will only cater for the obstacles you have been able to foresee. So, just trust yourself that when you get there, you're capable of figuring it out.

4.   Accept That Perfect Isn't Possible

You are going to be tempted to develop the "perfect" plan – after all, this is the rest of your life that you are mapping out – right? Again, a perfectly natural reaction but one you must resist. Whilst that attainment of perfection is an admirable aspiration it should not get in the way of acting.

Bill Gates, Co-founder of Microsoft, was well known for his philosophy of releasing products that were 85% (or higher) right. His belief was that trying to get the product to 100% right before it was launched would not work – mainly because the world was constantly moving, so by the time you got to 100% the world had moved and you slid back to 90% or 95%. Then there was that nasty element of competition – he was adamant that no competitor would beat him to market.

Whilst we can argue about the implications of this, you cannot argue with his success. Microsoft's success with the Windows operating system is testament to this philosophy – each time a new version was released any shortcomings or bugs would be fixed through a schedule of "updates"

Perfectionism is fear. Fear keeps us from acting. It's better to have something great IN THE WORLD than to have something perfect tucked away on your hard drive somewhere. People who are really successful aren't perfect, they're just doing it. Embrace imperfection like it's your best friend forever - because that's what separates the visible from the invisible.

There's a great article on dealing with perfectionism in the resources area of the support website (www.whencaniretire.com.au).

5.   Make Fear Your New Best Friend

Fear is part of everyone's story. Most people won't tell you about it, until they've reached some degree of success. I don't know about you, but I have lost count of the number of times I have heard, "I was so scared at first, but I did it, and it worked!" or variations thereof.

Once you get over your initial fears, more fears will crop up. If you ever STOP feeling anxious or fearful, you're probably not pushing the envelope enough. Fear is a natural reaction to risk and uncertainty.

Without risks, there's no reward, and whenever you take risks, it's human to feel nervous about it.

What matters most is that you're AWARE when fear is holding you back. In fact, when you learn to LISTEN to your fears, they can be your greatest ally in doing the right things. There's an old saying, "If it terrifies you, you should probably say yes." Identify what it is that you are afraid of and then undertake a risk analysis assessment using the tools in this book. It's amazing what a difference that makes in putting a fear into perspective.

If you are consistent about getting movement and making time for a positive mindset practice, whether that is through meditation, journaling or going for a gratitude walk. Positive thoughts tend to multiply, so even 5 minutes a day can have a great impact on your mindset.

Creating a confident mindset is the first step in providing your retirement lifestyle plan with the best possible environment for its implementation and success. Take these steps to believe in yourself, so you can inject that confidence into your plan and, as a result, enjoy the sort of lifestyle that will make you the envy of those around you.

Follow Your Plan

"If you don't design your own life plan, chances are you'll fall into someone else's plan. And guess what they have planned for you? Not much."
Jim Rohn

A formal plan is a documented process designed to commit us to specific actions for the future in order to improve our chances of successfully reaching a goal or set of goals.

That's what your retirement lifestyle plan is and what forms a large part of this book's content. However, not every plan leads to success. Here's a few thoughts to consider about formal planning;

- Not everyone who starts the planning process completes it. Developing a plan requires some hard work and decision making – not everyone is up for that.
- Of those who complete the planning process, not all will be successful.
- Those who are successful will experience setbacks along the way.

Staying focused on any complex task is hard – and planning is complex (as you will have already gathered by reading through section two of the book). At the start of the planning process you are certainly going to be motivated - but you are going to find that your motivation wanes over time. We get caught up, stuck, frustrated, overloaded, overworked, distracted, and we simply just veer off track. Clearly, it's hard to stay focused when we have so much going on in our lives. Or is it?

When your obligations stretch you thin, and you're pulled in every which direction, it's easy to let life overwhelm you. It's easy to get inundated by emergencies and crises that feel almost unavoidable, so losing that all-important focus feels largely, well, unimportant. Yet, in the back of our minds, we know that those excuses will only take us so far. Yes, it's easy to let life get the best of us, but it's not okay to veer so far off track that we forget what we truly wanted out of life and why we really wanted it. Staying focused on the goals that your plan is based on is not only important, it's crucial.

I know that I have become frustrated with my progress towards some of my goals in the past. Very little of what I have ever wanted to achieve was simple or easy. But, then again, I wouldn't have wanted it as much if it were simple and easy. Big goals are usually so far off from where we are that it can almost be frightening. Understanding that life is going to get in your way, you are going to need to be able to refocus on your retirement lifestyle goals – time, after time, after time.

You need a system to be able to do this consistently. There are methods and techniques that you can implement to help you avoid getting side-tracked or veering off course too much. The key here is to be aware that a loss of focus is going to happen and to have a strategy that will allow you to refocus and stay on course. The good news is that I am going to help you with this.

I am going to show you how you can stay focused on your goals so that you can achieve the things that you want to achieve in your retirement - rather than being stuck in the status quo for another day, week, month, or even year.

Here are eight very powerful methods that you can employ to help maintain your focus to be able to follow your plan. You can employ one or many, depending on your own, individual, circumstances.

1. Condense Your Plan

By the time you complete your retirement lifestyle plan it will be both comprehensive and lengthy. Whilst you will be referring to it a lot, it will be likely that you will not refer to it all the time.

You need to have a condensed version which retains the essence of the plan's intent but not all of its detail. The condensed version will become a document that is brief and that will provide you with a "snapshot" to remind you of both where you are trying to get to and where you are now.

When I condense a plan – be it for myself or a client – I try to make it no more than five A4 pages. My preference though, where possible, is to condense it down to a single page.

You can only achieve this if you have SMART goals and measurable KPI's

Here's what I include in my condensed version;

- Vision summary – no more than a couple of paragraphs on what my retirement plan lifestyle is going to look like. This should be a window to your motivation – your "why"
- Goals – my high priority goals (no more than three to five) and a maximum of five lower priority goals which relate to the current 18 month horizon
- KPI's – only those that relate to the goals (above)
- Copy of schedule of activities for the next 90 days (on a separate piece of paper)

Armed with this document you will be able to re-focus anytime you feel that you might have become distracted and, because the condensed plan is so brief, it is not intimidating to pick up and browse through it.

2. Revisit Your Why

You need to be able to connect to your why often. Life is full of distractions and it is easy to get trapped in the day to day without fully appreciating what that is doing to you. Being clear about your why and being able to access it as a reminder is a critical tool in being able to maintain focus on your "big picture" and plan.

3. Take Back Control Of Your Time

This will be especially important when you are in the process of transitioning from your working life to your retirement lifestyle. This is the time when you will still have commitments that compete with each other for your attention – you still need to work (and live up to your responsibilities in that space) but you also need to be able carry out relevant actions to move your retirement plan closer to activation.

Simply putting off actions from your retirement lifestyle plan to make way for your current day to day is not the answer because, at some point, your retirement is going to happen, and you need to be well prepared for it. Being in control of your time is difficult - but essential if you are going to be able to maintain focus. However, this book is not about managing your time – you can find resources that will help you do this on the support website (www.whencanire-tire.com.au). I would also recommend that you take a look at David Allen's book, "Getting Things Done" as it is an excellent resource for taking back control of your time.

4. Remember Your KPI's

We discussed KPI's in section two, they were also mentioned in method one – "Condense Your Plan".

KPI's are the milestones by which you can evaluate if you are on track or not. The basic premise here is that you can assume that, if you are achieving your KPI's, then you can safely assume that all of the other myriad details that your retirement lifestyle plan covers are also being achieved. Having a few KPI's, as opposed to dozens of little details, makes it easier to keep focused. Anytime that you feel a sense of overwhelm because so much is going on, you just check those KPI's and, if all is good in that department, the rest will likely take of itself.

5. Regularly Review Your Condensed Plan

Due to your condensed plan is no more than five pages it is easy to review it. If, as a consequence of that review, you need more details around an issue or element, you can get these by looking at your master plan (from which the condensed version was created).

Decide a review frequency which suits your circumstances but make this a regular thing that is not some once in a while activity but a part of your entire process. It's a good idea to schedule this review in your diary or mark it off on your calendar. This provides you with some discipline around the review process.

6.   Analyse Your Progress Regularly

A review of your condensed plan keeps you focused on your bigger picture. Analysing progress forces you to evaluate how you are doing in terms of whether you are meeting your KPI's. If you are not, identify why and engage some of the alternate strategies contained in your Master Plan.

Regular analysis means that you will be able to act on deviations before they become critical issues and will also afford you a wider range of options to reach a remedy. This early intervention is always less costly and less stressful than when left until the last moment.

7.   Deal With Procrastination

I pointed out some of the reasons as to why we procrastinate earlier in the book and we will be covering this element some more shortly. However, it is important to understand the negative impact that procrastination has on your productivity which, in turn, impacts on your ability to deliver on your plan's goals.

We all procrastinate, and you will never totally eliminate this barrier to productivity, but you can minimise it and its impacts through understanding the signs of procrastination and what you can do about it. More on this in the next chapter.

8.   Apply Motivational Techniques

Your final method for staying focused on your retirement lifestyle plan is to implement some motivational techniques to help keep you on track. When you find yourself lacking in motivation you have to shift your focus.

Anyone who has made a New Year's resolution knows that this is easier said than done! If you want something badly enough, you'll do what it takes to push forward, but for how long? What happens when you get frustrated or you have a bad day? What if you suffer a major setback or failure? What helps to keep you going? What helps to motivate you?

Understand what it is that motivates you – when do you feel energised and why? Is it watching a motivational TED Talk video, listening to some favourite music, remembering a positive event in your life, reading some inspirational quotes? The reality is that only you can lift yourself to the required level of motivation.

Of course, you have your retirement lifestyle vision, plan and goals which should go a long way to helping you re-energise your motivation levels.

Here are some motivation "hacks" to help you on your way:
- Find an accountability partner.
- Visualize the positive outcomes.
- Celebrate your achievements.
- Introduce some fun.
- Set realistic expectations.
- Collect inspiring quotes

Make no mistake, you are going to meet some resistance, but this isn't the end of the road. The most successful people in the world have failed hard, and they've failed often, before they achieved success. Be cautious about failure but don't be afraid of it.

Most importantly don't allow it to let you lose your focus on your goals. Keep pushing, keep going, and, in the words of Tim Allen's character, Commander Taggart, in the movie "Galaxy Quest " - "Never give up! Never surrender!"

Celebrating Small Wins

"I've found that small wins, small projects, small differences often make huge differences."
Rosabeth Moss Kanter

The process of shifting your life from a work focus to a retirement focus is confronting – it is not something that happens by itself (even though many people believe that it does).

Planning for this momentous event in your life is the sensible thing to do but that planning process is also not easy – nor is it straightforward. You are going to have to seriously challenge just about everything you have been taking for granted for most of your life. Habits that have served you well up to this point will become less and less productive and will need to change if you are going to have any hope of your longevity bonus not turning into a living hell.

It follows suit that, with all of the above, the journey ahead will be challenging. Yes, retirement is a time to look forward to – a time when you are going to be able to exercise more control over your life – but you need to prepare for it. As I have stated many times in this book, if your retirement lifestyle dream is going to materialise for you, you are going to have to prepare yourself and prepare yourself well.

To paraphrase the Chinese philosopher Lao-Tzu, "the longest journey always starts with the first few steps". Your planning for your retirement lifestyle is such a journey, a journey you will need to take a few steps at a time. That journey will be challenging and there are going to be times along the way when you will seriously doubt your ability to make this work for you -in the manner you want it to. This is why you need to celebrate the numerous "small wins" you are going to have along the way.

In his book, "The Power of Habits", Charles Duhigg uses the term "small wins" to refer to small behaviour changes that can set off a chain reaction of more and better changes.

This "small wins" idea is powerful because it is always easier to take the smaller steps that lead to small wins than it is to attempt massive strides for big wins. The great news is that, by taking the right small steps, you are, ultimately, moving yourself closer to those big wins too!

Instead of trying to do many things differently, you can always focus on doing just "one thing differently," and, having mastered that, move on to the next and the next. In no time, you will be looking back and surprising yourself as to how much progress you have made! Just make sure to celebrate the "small wins" that taking "small steps" affords you. Why?

Every small win you achieve gives you a shot of dopamine - that feel-good brain chemical that is linked with motivation. Better still, a series of small wins provides you with a constant supply of dopamine, which is released during goal-oriented behaviour and upon achieving a goal. Not only does the small win mentality build confidence, these "shots" of dopamine are going to make you feel good and will provide you with added motivation to keep moving forward. In our day to day lives, we normally perform some activities which qualify as wins. They could be as small as remembering to eat healthy or performing well in a particular job task. For most of us, these small victories go largely unnoticed. However, we are quick to notice any mistakes or shortcomings that we could make during our day. While it is important to notice our mistakes (so as we can correct them), we should not ignore those small wins. It is really about catching yourself doing something right, rather than dwelling on what hasn't gone according to plan.Get into the habit of noticing your small wins – which is best classified as any activity which you do successfully but weren't sure you could actually pull off. This is going to vary from person to person. Small wins do not change the world - but they can put a smile on your face and help you gain some confidence!

Here are a few tips to help you shift to a mindset where you are catching yourself doing something right:

- Notice the win. Pay attention – have you just accomplished a task or made headway on a high priority goal that you worried about achieving?
- Get excited

Children get very excited about small things. This keeps them happy and enthusiastic about life. As we grow up, we become harder to impress and it becomes difficult to get excited about things that do not qualify as big and significant. Sometimes, we fail to get excited by small things in a bid to impress other adults. If you are excited about some small thing you have achieved, let it show. If you feel happy because you were finally able to do that small thing that you have struggled with for a while, then get excited about it. Bask in the victory of having achieved it and it will increase your level of happiness.

- Communicate your small wins

We humans are social beings - we communicate with each other to share ideas or moments. So, when you experience a small victory, you should tell someone who cares about it. Find ways to verbalize your small win and tell it to someone else. This will create a little celebration party for you and others.

- Establish habits which help you to make small wins every day

For you to have something to celebrate, you have to make an effort. To make progress on a daily basis, you need to learn how to win consistently. This can only be accomplished using habits.

Habits are activities which you perform without thinking about it. They come naturally to you because you have programmed your mind and body to suit them.

- Live in the present moment and acknowledge it

Whenever we are focused on the future there is a danger that we can take the present moment for granted. We think that the little activities that we perform presently do not affect us and our trajectory. But they do. Day to day moments are the ones which add up over time.

- Reward yourself

You should always reward yourself for achieving something – no matter how small that something is. A reward is anything that brings you pleasure.

Take the time to reward yourself. This can be a favourite food, some time watching your favourite show, some ice cream or chocolate.

When you celebrate those small wins with a reward it motivates you to maintain focus and keep winning. It is a way to program yourself for long term achievement and happiness.

- Don't overly pressure yourself

Ever since our early school days, we have worked with deadlines and the pressure to do our best. We carry this habit into adulthood and often manifest unrealistic expectations.

We also have a tendency to focus on what we haven't completed (successfully) rather than what we have – this puts us under pressure. A little pressure is good for us but too much will burn us out.

- Share your plan

Your retirement lifestyle is not going to be solitary – at least I hope not! Share it with the people close to you who will be sharing this life-style you are working towards creating.

Being able to celebrate small wins with others magnifies the impact of those celebrations – and that's a good thing.

It is important to stay motivated for this journey towards your retirement lifestyle and the most effective way to maintain that motivation is by celebrating small wins. When you learn how to celebrate your small wins you are going to find it much easier to stay on track to reach those high priority goals.

The Habit Principle

"Ninety-nine percent of the failures come from people who have the habit of making excuses."
George Washington Carver

We are all creatures of habit – in fact we are hard wired to develop habits as much as possible!

What is a habit?

In simple terms a habit is a response to our environment which results in a usual way of behaving or a tendency that someone has settled into. Our brains rely on the formation of habits to simplify our lives and to conserve energy. Habits are formed as a response to our environment and the situations we face on regular basis. Whenever we are faced with a task or situation our brains instinctively ask the question, "have we faced this before?" if the answer to that is yes, the next questions our brains formulate are, "what did we do?" and, "did that (action or series of actions) work?" If the answers to those questions are satisfactory, we simply rinse and repeat. The logic being it worked last time so should work this time.

If we are facing a new situation, we have to go into problem solving and decision making mode and that takes both time and energy. Habits save us on both of those fronts.

You see, our brains are our single most energy intensive organ. It is estimated that around 20% of our daily energy consumption is by our brains (more if we are thinking intensively). Our brain is programmed to conserve energy wherever possible. This is one of the reasons why we put off making difficult decisions – the energy those decisions require is substantial, so we are looking for any way at all to conserve that.

Habits afford us the opportunity to function in an energy efficient manner because they represent learned behaviours that we don't really need to think too hard about. In fact, each and every day you are doing things that you don't even notice because you do them so frequently you just don't pay them any attention. Take your daily routine as a case in point. The first hour that you are awake you engage a number of behaviours that you do without thinking;

- When you awake, do you think about which side of the bed you will get out of, which leg you will place on the floor first? No, you simply get up (even when you don't want to!) – nothing to think about there!

- Whilst you may think for a while about what to wear, you will give no thought to the order and manner by which you get dressed. You'll step into your underwear and put on your clothes without a thought and yet there are numerous decisions being made automatically (through habit) – do I put my underwear over my right leg first or the left? Do I use my right or left hand or both?

- How you get into the shower presents choices you also will not think about. Nor will you give any thought as to how you will wash and dry yourself

These "micro" decisions, and dozens more besides, are being made by you without a thought and each and every one of them is saving you time, effort and energy! Imagine how much longer your morning routine would take if you had to give each and every step some serious thought.

Habits also help us to be more capable and confident – each time you undertake the same task you get better at it, as you get better at it you become more confident and you get faster at performing that task. These things are what make habits essential, the good side, so to speak.

Habits do have a dark side. Habits are born out of responses to our environment and our environment changes. Habits, though, do not change so readily.

Think about it – when you are good at doing something (because you have been doing it for a while) it makes you feel good about yourself; it also provides you with a sense of self-worth. So, you are not about to let all of that go in a hurry!

Habits outlive their usefulness and you have to be constantly reviewing whether a habit or set of habits has passed their use by date – before they become so unproductive as to result in undesirable outcomes. In a nutshell, every habit starts with a psychological pattern called a "habit loop" which is a three-part process;

1. There's a cue, or trigger, that tells your brain to go into automatic mode and let a behaviour unfold.
2. Then follows the routine, which is the behaviour itself.
3. Lastly is the reward: something that your brain likes that helps it remember the "habit loop" in the future.

Good habits are those that are continuing to provide a payoff either in terms of a reward or productivity or both. Bad habits are those which we continue despite environmental changes that render the habit non-productive.

Neuroscientists have traced our habit-making behaviours to a part of the brain called the Basal Ganglia, which also plays a key role in the development of emotions, memories and pattern recognition. Decisions, meanwhile, are made in a different part of the brain called the Prefrontal Cortex. But as soon as a behaviour becomes automatic, the decision-making part of your brain no longer plays an active role in the process.

What your brain is attempting to achieve is to work less and less on repetitive tasks which is a real advantage as it means that you have all of this mental activity you can devote to something else. That's why it's easy — while driving for example — to completely focus on something else: like the radio, or a conversation you're having, or both!

222 • DENNIS HALL

It's not just individuals that call on habits to save time, energy and effort. Organisations do the same thing – it's just that they call their habits "Processes" and "Systems" and we all know how hard it can be to change those!

Okay, so we know that changing habits is hard, but we also know that, with retirement, there are going to be a lot of habits that will pass their use by date. So, how to change?

On average, it takes more than two months before a new behaviour becomes fully automatic. You can establish a habit in around twenty one days but to cement that habit into an automatic routine will require the habit to be actively engaged for up to another month or more.

This is not a hard and fast rule though - how long it takes a new habit to form can vary widely depending on the behaviour, the person, and the circumstances.

Here are eight steps to follow to change a habit which has outlived its usefulness:

1. Cut yourself some slack. Habits are hard to change because, well, they're habits, and you are used to them
2. Identify the underlying cause – what is the trigger?
3. Deal with the real issue
4. Write it down
5. Get yourself a support person. Changing a habit is going to involve setbacks so you will need support through that, and you will also need someone to hold you accountable.
6. Identify an alternate behaviour/response that you intend to replace the bad habit with.
7. Give yourself enough time.
8. Allow for slips (and refer to step one).

The Enemy Within

"It is better to conquer yourself than to win a thousand battles. Then the victory is yours. It cannot be taken from you, not by angels or by demons, heaven or hell."
Buddha

The hardest work you are going to need to do in retirement is to work on yourself. You have a lifetime of bad habits to deal with and some of these will be tough to eliminate (refer playing victim & other examples). If you are like the majority of people, you have been used to having work as a mechanism that keeps you honest – it has kept you moving. Think about it...

How many times in your life have you got out of bed and got dressed only because you have a job to go to and, if you didn't turn up you just didn't get paid (and those bills just kept on coming)?

We all have those days and, sometimes, we succumb to our lack of motivation and stay in bed; but what happens when you have one of those days when you are retired? What are you going to do to give yourself the motivation to get up and face the world?

What are you going to do to prevent "one of those days" turning into another, and another and another – before you know it, one of those days turns into your new normal and now you are in real trouble! Hopefully, through reading this book, you are going to be able to find your "why" and that will provide you with the spark you need to keep going when you just don't feel like it.

Don't get me wrong – I am not suggesting that you try to stay in high achievement mode every waking hour, but you do need to become self-driven. The expectations of a work environment only ever provided extrinsic motivation to keep going. You quickly need to be able to make that motivation intrinsic.

We all have within us the tendency to "self-sabotage" – to actually engage in behaviours which work against us achieving our goals. Steven Pressfield sums it up beautifully in his book, "The War of Art", when he talks about "resistance";

"...In other words, any act that rejects immediate gratification in favour of long term growth, health or integrity. Or, expressed another way, any act that derives from our higher nature instead of our lower. Any of these will elicit resistance."

Resistance refers to the internal struggle we have between working towards attainment of longer term aspirations and the temptation to give up or to do nothing or to just put it off for a short time (more on that shortly).

Pressfield identifies the characteristics of resistance as being;

- Originating internally – it is self-generated and self-perpetuated
- It's sneaky – it will use any method to divert you and any logic to fool you
- It is unyielding – It cannot be reasoned with (because it knows all of your arguments). It is an engine of (your) destruction
- Resistance doesn't care about you. It's a force of nature and it acts objectively
- It does not deviate – resistance always takes you away from what your true aims are. This is its weakness – whenever you feel the strongest urge to not do something it's a sure sign that resistance is at work so stay on course!
- Its universal – everyone experiences resistance. Successful people manage to beat it

- Resistance never sleeps – which means you can't either. Be ever vigilant
- Resistance means business
- Resistance is driven by fear
- Resistance is at its most powerful when you are closest to your goal

The most common form of resistance is procrastination, so let's take a look at what that looks like and, most importantly, what you can do about it

Procrastination

"Never do today what you can put off until tomorrow" (Anon)

I covered procrastination in Section two of the book in the chapter, "The Devil Is In The Details". All I want to do here is provide you with some more tools that you can apply in your battle to defeat this beast.

Tool number one is referred to as the "Five Whys Technique" and it is excellent in providing a self-analysis framework to identify a root cause. Here's what it looks like;

First, identify the whys – ask yourself why you procrastinate over this issue or task. There is a questioning strategy that works extremely well when it comes to identifying root causes in such instances – and it is these root causes you have to identify, otherwise you will just be dealing with symptoms and the situation will keep occurring

Here's how it works:

A. Starting with the issue/task you are procrastinating over, you ask yourself;
B. "Why am I procrastinating over this?" (First Why)
C. Next, you ask a question relating to that answer (second Why)
D. Then, you use that answer to formulate your next question (third Why)
E. The answer from that question provides you with the basis for the next question (fourth Why)
F. This prompts the final question (fifth Why)

Here's an example of what that might look like;

1. Why am I putting off starting my retirement plan? (first Why)

   A: It looks like hard work

2. Why does it look like hard work? (second Why)

   A: There's a lot to consider?

3. Why does having a lot to consider intimidate you? (third Why)

   A: I don't know where to start

In the above example we don't need a fourth or fifth "Why?" This is because we have identified the root cause at "why" number three – not knowing where to start is the real issue here and that can be solved by simply breaking down all of the tasks associated with the plan and tackling them one at a time – the order in which you do that can be determined by following a plan template or by actioning one element at a time – if it becomes obvious you need to tackle a different element as you go through this you simply pause on one and start the other.

Whilst this "to and from" approach is time consuming; it at least provides you with progress – you will, ultimately, complete the plan and can then go from there. Using the "Five Whys" technique to identify root causes of blockages is only one way of stimulating forward movement. The important thing is to do something - it's all about making sure you have the right mindset and approach. Let's looks at some of the other ways you can achieve this:

Tool number two is the "Fifteen minute" rule. Simply grab your smartphone (or any other device with a timer) and set it to 15 minutes.

The concept is that fifteen minutes is a number that's too small to fail at. We can all do something for fifteen minutes. Commit to doing whatever it is that you've been putting off for fifteen minutes (or at least a part of it), no more.

Once the fifteen minutes are up, you can choose to stop. Or, if momentum is on your side, keep going.

What you'll find is that, after fifteen minutes, you'll usually want to keep going even if you stop, you at least broke the seal. You stopped procrastinating, even if it was only for a short while. Since habits take time to form or break, this is an important step in the art of habit formation.

Neural pathways, which comprise those habit channels in our brains, etch deeper and deeper over time. When left unabated, they simply continue etching deeper. And, the deeper that channel etches, the harder it is to break a habit. That's why procrastination, and any other bad habit, becomes exponentially harder to stop over time. So, the fifteen minute-rule is a perfect pattern disruption technique.

Tool number three is often referred to as the Eisenhower or Urgent/Important Matrix. It was developed by Dwight D. Eisenhower (former President of the USA) but was "re-introduced" to the mainstream by Dr. Stephen Covey in his book "The 7 Habits of Highly Effective People". It is a powerful decision making tool, as it helps you to decide on and prioritise your tasks based on urgency and importance while sorting out less urgent and less important tasks. It is based on the principle that, "what is important is seldom urgent and what is urgent is seldom important."

Using a simple grid, it defines tasks according to their importance and urgency:

Quadrant 1 - Crises - URGENT and IMPORTANT
Quadrant 2 - Goals and Planning - NON-URGENT and IMPORTANT
Quadrant 3 - Interruptions - URGENT and NOT IMPORTANT
Quadrant 4 - Distractions - NOT URGENT and NOT IMPORTANT
What do we mean here by Important and Urgent?

- Urgent Tasks: cause us to react, we stop what we're currently doing and work on the urgent task instead.
- Important Tasks: lead us towards our overall mission or goals and these key actions often require planning, organization and initiative.

The tool allows us to consciously give priority to our most important tasks and to plan and delegate so that we deal with problems BEFORE they become urgent crises and to become aware of our interruptions and distractions so that we can reduce or eliminate them. Using this tool will empower you to manage your limited time resources so that you are able to get your priority tasks done in a more enjoyable and less stressful way.

There's a template you can download and use in the resources area of the support website; (www.whencaniretire.com.au).

The matrix looks like the illustration in figure nine.

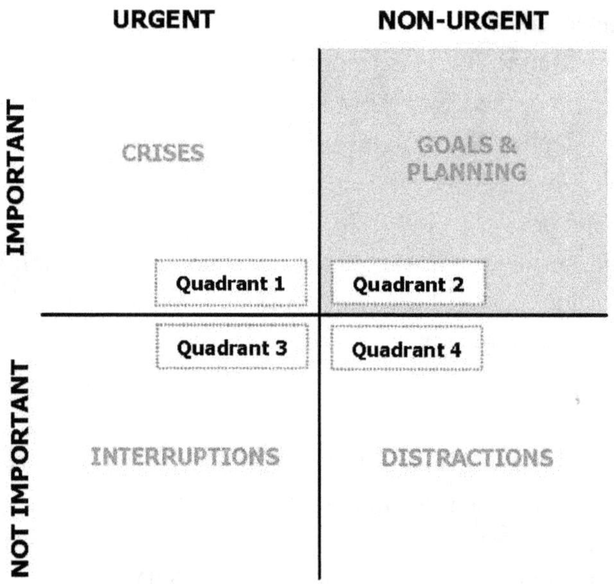

	URGENT	NON-URGENT
IMPORTANT	CRISES Quadrant 1	GOALS & PLANNING Quadrant 2
NOT IMPORTANT	Quadrant 3 INTERRUPTIONS	Quadrant 4 DISTRACTIONS

Figure 9. You can find more information on this matrix on the support website (www.whencaniretire.com.au).

You will never totally eliminate resistance – it is internally hard wired within us – but you can learn to recognise the signs of it being at work with you and develop strategies to deal with it. Focus on your energy and attention levels as you can exert more control on these areas - it's where your productivity action is!

Here are five questions you can ask yourself when you feel resistance trying to divert your attention;

1. What matters in the present? Priorities evolve over time and it is important to recognise this, rather than acting on priorities from the past.
2. What actions can I take today and moving forward (tomorrow, in a week's time) that most reflect my priorities?
3. What are the priorities of the people who are around me and who matter to me and do they align with my priorities?
4. What is consuming my attention that doesn't reflect my priorities and how can I rectify this?
5. Who can I share my priorities with to receive the support I need to act?

Resistance is not exclusively an internal element. You are going to also meet resistance from other people. So let's explore that in the next chapter.

The Enemy Without

"A friend wearing a mask can cause more damage than an enemy without one."
Anon

In the previous chapter we examined why we self-sabotage and what we can do about it. However, this is not the only way that our plans can hit roadblocks. The people around us can also be a source of resistance and, given that these people are likely to be family members and close personal friends (we are talking about a retirement lifestyle after all!) if you want to preserve those relationships, it is going to be important to be able to identify and deal with any resistance.

Let's begin by exploring why people tend to resist change. Here are ten of the main motivators behind that resistance:

1. Misunderstanding
   When the reason for the change is unclear — If people do not understand the need for change you can expect resistance. Especially from those who strongly believe the current way of doing things works well.

2. Fear of the unknown — One of the most common reasons for resistance is fear of the unknown. People will only take active steps toward the unknown if they genuinely believe – and perhaps more importantly, feel – that the risks of standing still are greater than those of moving forward in a new direction.

3. Lack of confidence — This is a fear people will seldom admit. But sometimes, change necessitates changes in

skills, and some people will feel that they won't be able to make the transition very well.

4. Connected to the old way — If you ask people to do things in a new way, as rational as that new way may seem to you, you will be setting yourself up against all that hard wiring, all those emotional connections to the old way – and that's not trivial.

5. Low trust — When people don't believe that they, or you, can competently manage the change there is likely to be resistance.

6. Poor communication — It's self-evident isn't it? Adopting a retirement lifestyle is going to mean some big changes. In such instances there's no such thing as too much communication.

7. Changes to routines — When we talk about comfort zones, we're really referring to routines (habits). We love them. They make us secure. There's bound to be resistance whenever change requires us to do things differently.

8. Exhaustion/Saturation — Don't mistake compliance for acceptance. People who are overwhelmed by continuous or too much change resign themselves to it and go along with the flow. You have them in body, but you do not have their hearts. Motivation is low.

9. Change in the status quo — Resistance can also stem from perceptions of the change that people hold. For example, people who feel they'll be worse off at the end of the change are unlikely to give it their full support. Similarly, if people believe the change favours other people over themselves there may be (unspoken) anger and resentment.

10. Benefits and rewards — When the benefits and rewards for making the change are not seen as adequate for the trouble involved.

No matter what the relationship you have, make no mistake – when it comes to lifestyle changes, people are always going to assess the risks and benefits in terms of what those changes mean to them, not to you – even though they may communicate their resistance in terms of having your best interests at heart.

Their first (internal) questions are likely to focus on two domains;

1. How will it affect them?
2. How will it affect their relationship (with you)?

Their reactions will either be;

1. Covert

    They appear to be onside and supportive but, secretly, they resent what lies ahead and will work subtly against your plans

2. Overt

    They are not onside and will let you know it – usually pretty quickly!

By far, the easiest reactions to deal with are the overt ones – you know where they stand, they have let you know where they stand, and you have the opportunity to work with them to allay their reservations and get them onside.

Dealing with covert resistance is far more challenging because, by its very nature, you are often unaware of its existence until a situation arises where that resistance becomes evident. That usually only happens over a period of time, where things have been getting in the way of you making progress on a particular issue or series of issues. You finally put two and two together and ask the person (or persons) involved what is going on and they confess their reservations.

Now you can have a conversation around that, allay their fears/reservations and, hopefully, get them back onside. That's the easy way covert resistance is dealt with.

The more difficult, and much more prevalent, way is that the person (or persons) involved continues to deny that there's any issue at all. In which case a different approach becomes necessary – more on that shortly!

Whether you are dealing with an overt or covert reaction, the first thing you need to identify is the cause of their reaction. Chances are high that it will be one of the ten main motivators for resistance to change that I outlined earlier.

Once you have identified the cause (and it can be a combination of the ten, as opposed to a single cause) you need to have a conversation with the person (or persons) involved. Make no mistake, these conversations can be challenging – depending on the relationship that you have and the issue (cause) at hand.

This book is not about how to have difficult conversations - and there is a real skill involved in having these conversations successfully (defined as reaching a resolution without permanent damage to the relationship) - but if you search online using the phrase "difficult conversations" you will get all the information you are going to need. I have included an introduction on this topic in the resource area of the support website that will at least allow you to get started (www.whencaniretire.com.au).

What do you do when someone you know is covertly resisting but they keep denying it and their relationship is important to you?

I would recommend that you give them at least two opportunities to admit to their resistance. Choose your time and place to have the conversations and space those conversations (based on separate incidents) a few days apart. These conversations should be approached gently, giving them the opportunity to explain their behaviour and, in so doing, allowing them to express their concerns (which will provide insights as to the cause of the resistance).

However, if this does not result in you being able to identify the cause(s) – they simply refuse to acknowledge their behaviours or simply rely on denial – then you have to be prepared to confront them. To do this you are going to have to have irrefutable evidence, which you will use in the conversation to show them that denial is no longer acceptable.

You can be certain that this will result in a more volatile exchange between you and them - and it is likely that the person (or persons)

234 • DENNIS HALL

you have such a conversation with will try to engage in emotional be-haviours rather than rational ones. As long as you are able to maintain your composure, the conversation will bring out into the open the cause of the resistance which you can then assess in terms of how best to deal with it.

Do not attempt to resolve the issue in that conversation. Rather, once you have identified what you believe to be the cause, politely withdraw from the conversation and give both yourself and them some time to cool down before having another conversation around resolv-ing the issue(s) associated with the cause(s) you previously identified. You do not want an argument (although it might appear that they do), which is why you have to remain composed throughout. An argument results when both parties lose their tempers (and composure and per-spective). Arguments damage relationships over time and you want to preserve the relationship at all costs. Take my situation when my wife and I had decided that we would embark on a two year adventure to Germany......

My wife's mother, Barbara, seemed to be fine with our decision when we told her of our plans in early 2014. Yes, she was surprised and a little taken aback, but she seemed genuinely happy for us. As time marched on we could tell that something was bothering her about us leaving. She didn't actually come out and say anything directly – it was more a hint here and there and periods of silence that alerted us to the fact that she may have not been as in full support of our move as we thought.

Things came to a head in late May 2015 when I purchased a 20 foot container to store those belongings of ours that we were keeping but not taking with us. We had agreed with Iris's sister and husband that we would store the container at their property during our absence. They have five acres of space and a large shed where the container could easily fit. This storage option had been discussed several times in Barbara's presence and she had never raised any concerns regarding it.

The container was delivered in mid-June - it had been raining quite heavily and, unfortunately, the ground was so soft that the delivery truck got bogged and couldn't place the container in the shed. We were going to have to figure a way to move it into position ourselves. By this time, we were living with Barbara in her four bedroom apartment as we had moved out of our Noosa home so as to get it ready for lease. The evening of the container delivery mishap I told Iris and Barbara about the situation.

Barbara's response was to say, "well, I really don't know why you don't just store your things in my garage downstairs!" Barbara has a double garage and only uses one side. The other side was more than large enough to store those belongings we were keeping. Iris and I were gobsmacked! At no point leading up to this moment had Barbara suggested her garage as a storage option – which we would have had no problem with as it would have saved us the cost of the container.

I was going to press ahead with using the container (as we had already paid for it) but, later that evening, Iris suggested we should go with Barbara's offer as it would make her feel more secure about us actually coming back to Australia, as opposed to deciding to remain in Germany permanently. That's when I had my lightbulb moment and realised that Barbara was not so keen on us going at all and a lot of "little" things started to make sense.

To give this some context for you; Barbara and her husband Herman (who unfortunately passed away in 2006) had come to Australia from Germany with their two young girls in 1972 for a two year adventure – and then stayed permanently.

When we had told her that we were going to Germany for a two year adventure she put two and two together and came up with five! Fortunately, I was able to sell the container we had bought, albeit for a lower price than we paid but we didn't take too much of a financial hit and, to be honest, the peace of mind that moving our stuff into her garage gave Barbara was more than worth it. In her mind Barbara felt more confident that we would return because our stuff was in her garage. I should have recognised her covert resistance earlier but, with everything else that was going on at the time, I didn't. Another lesson learned!

This type of fall back option, if you do not want to run the risk of damaging a relationship, is worth considering – to change an aspect or aspects of your plan that involve the covert resistance of a person (or persons) so that their resistance is no longer an issue. Of course, that is not always possible, but it is worth considering.

Remember, in all of this, your retirement lifestyle plan will involve people who are crucial to your plan's success and your life moving forward. These are the people who are more important than the plan itself and, realistically, should be involved in practically every step of your plan's development. Then there are the people who you want to continue to have in your life beyond retirement but who are not crucial to its success. These are the people who you might share at least some aspects of your plan with but whom you would not involve in its formulation.

Being aware of resistance in others and developing strategies to deal with that will enable you to implement your plan with far less heartache and a far higher likelihood of success

Push Your Boundaries

"If you always put a limit on everything you do, physical or anything else. It will spread into your work and into your life. There are no limits. There are only plateaus, and you must not stay there, you must go beyond them."
Bruce Lee

We are all capable of much more than we imagine, and I have gone to great lengths to emphasise that your mindset is going to be the single biggest contributor (or roadblock) to where you see yourself in retirement. Limiting your own success was a concept that was relatively alien to me until I was thirty years old. Fortunately, I had a CEO and a mentor at a company I was the state sales manager for in NSW, in 1986, that were determined to expand my thinking.

That company was called Jetset Tours, and at the time it was Australia's largest travel organisation. I had been with the company for a little over 18 months when a restructure of operations provided me with the opportunity to relocate to the company's head office in Melbourne as the Victoria/Tasmania Sales Development Manager. The move provided me with the added responsibility of overseeing the sales function for two additional divisions within the company. It was a huge step up for me - more of a giant leap really, and I have to confess that there were times in my first six months in the role when I wondered, "what the hell have I done?!"Fortunately, one of the company's senior managers, Peter, took me under his wing and provided me with some much needed support & guidance. This enabled me to weather the initial storm and settle into the role successfully.

Less than a year in however, and the CEO asked me if I was prepared to take on the planning and execution of a national conference
for a newly formed group of retail travel agents that were to expand
the company's brand position in the retail travel market. The conference was, basically, the launch of this new retail branded group which
comprised over 350 independently owned travel agents who were to
become known and branded as Jetset Travel Centres.

My brief was to manage the whole thing - establish the conference
agenda, source venue, secure key industry partner participation and
achieve a minimum attendance of 65% of the travel agencies that
formed the group – oh, and to do all of that on a cost neutral basis
(which for the uninitiated is corporate speak for, "it was not to cost the
company anything")!

Now, when I say that the CEO asked me if I was prepared to do
this, he was not expecting me to say no. In fact, he was a very difficult
man to say no to (and live to tell the tale anyhow!). I expressed my
reservations as to my ability to successfully lead the project - not the
least of which was my lack of logistical expertise, but he was having
none of it and I got the distinct impression that to flatly refuse was not
a good career move.

Having just settled into an almost manageable routine with my
State Sales Development role, I was back in turmoil – not only organising the conference but also maintaining my regular responsibilities
at the same time. It was a hectic and, at times, highly stressful six
months but I managed to pull it off – it was one of the most successful
launches the company ever undertook, with over 90% of the Travel
Centre agencies attending (and providing embarrassingly good feedback) and it even ran at a small profit!

Now, when I say "I" managed to pull it off, it was a team effort. I
had some great people in my team (many of whom I am still in contact
with) and my mentor, Peter, was an absolute rock – especially in re-
moving some obstacles that were placed in my way by other, less col-
laborative, people in the organisation. Here's the thing, that
experience demonstrated to me that I was far more capable than I

thought I could ever be, and it shaped the rest of my career. Never again would I allow myself to be intimidated by any project, task or person.

My career (and life) mindset was changed forever and I owe that to Jetset's CEO – mind you, at the time I wasn't in a mood to thank him for throwing me in the deep end!

Know this – as you read these words you, too, are capable of much more than you think. Hold that thought as you consider what you want your retirement lifestyle to look like and dare to dream! Be prepared to push your boundaries, to challenge yourself. There is absolutely nothing wrong with taking calculated risks. The key word in that last sentence being "calculated". Approaching retirement is no time to be cavalier and throw caution to the wind. You simply do not have enough "wriggle" room to recover (financially) should things go horribly wrong. That sort of risk taking is strictly for those in their younger years! So, get ready to be daring but be prepared.

The process of establishing your retirement lifestyle plan is not complicated - so long as you understand that when you are driving your own car, you will get off course and sometimes find the new courses are better (keep going) or worse (get back on the old course).

It IS important to note that just because something feels better in the moment doesn't mean that ANYTHING is getting better. The measures are based on your chosen outcomes, which you measure against your KPI's. You determine what you REALLY want and NEED in life. You determine what accomplishments you want and need to have and do. You determine who you want to be.

Hopefully, the information in this book will provide you not only with the tools you need to prepare for your "longevity bonus", through a retirement lifestyle plan, but also the inspiration to actually get on the front foot with this. Retirement is going to happen for you (and everyone else) – whether you are prepared for it or not is entirely within your control.

So, You Have A Plan

"It Doesn't Matter Where You Came From. All That Matters Is Where You Are Going."
Brian Tracy

This has been one hell of a ride hasn't it? All that work in thinking about what you want your future to look like and then having to actually work out how you are going to make that happen!

Well, guess what? The fun hasn't even started yet! The really interesting part of all this is when you actually engage your plan by acting.

Whilst I know, from my own experience, how much work there is in putting a comprehensive plan together, I also know that it is totally worth it – you are, after all, looking to create a retirement lifestyle that you are set to enjoy for at least 15 years and hopefully a lot longer! Your plan is going to become your "Go to" document for everything you do once you complete and activate it. This is why the plan is so valuable – it will inform all of your decisions and actions from that point forward. No more wondering what you should do next, no more stressing over unknowns – simply utilise the plan to inform your decisions and actions.

How much action you are going to have to take to turn your plan into reality is going to depend on how far out from retirement your plan is activated and what sort of lifestyle you seek to achieve.

When my wife and I made the decision to pack up and move to Germany it took us two years from decision to implementation of the plan and a further 12 months to make the move.

However, our situation is not typical, and your situation is going to be different to ours (and most everyone else's too!). You could go from deciding what you desire your retirement lifestyle to be like, to completing a plan and activating it in less than 12 months or take three years or more – it's entirely up to you and your circumstances.

Some people are great at planning but not so great at implementation. Others struggle with developing a plan but are real go-getters when it comes to acting. It doesn't matter which camp you fall into – as long as you know which it is, you can take advantage of your strengths and put that little bit of extra effort into those areas you are not so good at.

Your plan is not a static reference document – it is meant to form the basis of the actions you are going to take moving forward – so that is what you are now going to have to do – TAKE ACTION!

All too often I see people put in a massive amount of effort into their planning and then they ease off when it comes to taking action – do not fall into that trap (it's another form of the resistance that Stephen Pressfield tells us about and that I covered earlier in the book). You will have no shortage of excuses for not implementing your retirement lifestyle plan: too little time, too many demands from existing responsibilities, bills to pay, don't have the resources, etc.

Maybe you're suffering from a lack of confidence which is preventing you from stepping out of your comfort zone. Perhaps you feel that you lack the skills required or you don't know where to turn for help. Is your desire for perfection preventing you from moving forward in case you make a mistake? Whatever the reason, you need to just deal with it and move on. If you have read this far you know that something has to change – you understand that if you continue to do what you've always done, you'll end up with the same predictable outcomes. Clearly, that is not what you want.

Have you ever been guilty of this? I know I have. What plans do you have right now that need to be implemented? What are you doing to turn them into reality? Remember when I detailed what procrastination is and how to deal with it?

Well, what most of us suffer from when we are not taking the action we need to in order to move closer to our goals, is a form of procrastination – so go back and re-read that and then decide what is one thing you can do right now to take a step forward? It may be hard going to begin with, and you may need to rinse and repeat that process over days, weeks or even months. However, if you take those initial, difficult, steps (no matter how small they may be) you will start to build momentum and self-belief, and this will see you through to completion.

The journey may be difficult, but it is going to be worth it – Here are a few steps for you to implement that should assist you in taking the action you need to turn your plan from a dream into reality:

- Keep focused on your why – this will help to motivate you
- Read and re-read your plan, especially your goals
- Discuss your challenges with your partner/significant other
- Identify just one thing to do now and do it. Then identify and do the next thing (next action strategy)
- Celebrate your wins – no matter how small
- Keep track of your KPI's
- If something's not working – change it. Implement plan B, C, D, etc – just don't change for change's sake. Be prepared to modify the plan – not your goals (they are set in concrete – remember resistance?) but your timelines and tactics need to be flexible (you have alternates for everything if you have followed my guidelines)
- Keep things real – challenge yourself but do not attempt the impossible
- Seek expert support – if your plumbing springs a leak you call in a plumber, even though you can probably look up how to fix it with a Google search. So, it stands to reason that if you are stuck in an area of your plan that you have little experience with, you should seek expert support.
- Access the support area of this book's companion website – it's totally free to everyone who has purchased the book

and it contains additional materials, templates, articles and guidelines that you will find extremely useful (www.whencaniretire.com.au).

Remember that no-one can eat an elephant in one bite, but anyone can do it one bite at a time. I guarantee you that your plan will not come to fruition exactly as you foretold it – you are going to hit unexpected hurdles and some of your ideas will not work as you envisioned, they would. These are not mistakes – they are lessons to be learned. When we are presented with the unexpected, what to do? Let's address that next.

Dealing With The Unexpected

"You have to take risks. We will only understand the miracle of life fully when we allow the unexpected to happen."
Paulo Coelho

As you move towards your retirement lifestyle, even as you are completing your retirement lifestyle plan, you are going to meet all kinds of surprises and unexpected events. Hopefully, most of them will be minor but sometimes they are major, or life shaking events of a very unpleasant nature, causing difficulties and problems, resulting in stress you could well do without! We all prefer to be in control of our lives – it's one of the reasons you are reading this book. We feel safer in a familiar environment, doing the same things every day, without interruptions or changes in our day to day. How do you cope with surprises and unexpected events?

- Do you become stressed?
- Do you panic?
- Do you get flustered?
- Do you become angry?

Many people find it difficult to cope with the unexpected, such as:

- You want to make a cup of coffee but discover that you ran out of coffee.
- When you arrive at the bus or train station in the morning to go to work, you find out that the bus or train will be delayed.

These are minor events, I know, but they are unexpected and can have a big impact on your mood. Then there are other kinds of surprises and expected events, such as:

- Arriving to the airport and discovering that your flight is being delayed
- Coming home from work and discovering that there is a leak in the water pipes.
- Getting unexpectedly fired from your job.
- Learning that someone close to you has fallen seriously ill.
- Losing money or possessions.
- Loss of a loved one.

These are just a few instances of surprises and unexpected events which life is full of and which can cause you anxiety and stress -affecting your mind, moods and behaviour. It is best to be prepared for them – that way they will not have the same level of impact on you and those around you.

Here are seven tips for dealing with unexpected events:

1. Acknowledge the fact that surprises and unexpected events are part of life and are unavoidable. When you do this, it will be easier to deal with whatever happens to you. Life is dynamic, not static. Change is a part of life, and with change comes the unexpected.

2. Your attitude/mindset is key. A positive attitude is an asset in unexpected situations. Not all unexpected events are negative. Sometimes, what seems like a problem, or even a disaster, could be a blessing in disguise. A negative event can awaken ambition, motivation, and persistence, which would lead to progress and success.

3. Always develop options or fallbacks with your plan, in case the first plans fail. This prevents you from falling into a state of helplessness, fear, and not knowing what to do next.

4. Pause and take a few deep breaths before responding to the unexpected (unless you are crossing the road and a car has appeared from nowhere and is bearing down on you!) Look at what has happened and assimilate the news. In

many cases, this might something of minor importance that is easy to cope with. Maybe what happened is temporary, or something that can be easily fixed – refer to your plan for options ideas.

5. If what happened is irreversible, what good would you gain by becoming angry, stressed or panicked? You would gain nothing. Instead of getting flustered and confused, angry or feeling helpless, it would be much more useful to think constructively where you are going from there. You need to think how to adjust to the new situation and either fix it, improve it, or make the most of it.

6. Do not focus on what you may have lost or dwell on thinking about the past. You can't change the past, but you can learn from it and move forward.

7. Do not allow your emotions to take over. This helps you take a step back from problems, surprises and unexpected events, and therefore, to be less affected by them. Being in control of your emotions will help you stay calm and in control of yourself, so you will be in a better position to think through and deal with whatever is happening.

You don't fail unless you give up – any hurdle can be overcome. You only have one life to live; with decisive action and persistence, you can overcome every unexpected event and obstacle in your way to achieve the retirement lifestyle that you desire.

Section Three Summary

This section was focused on putting your plan into action. Your actions will determine the success of your plan. Whilst the planning process itself is challenging and time consuming, taking action on it is likely to pose your most significant challenge. Here's where the rubber really hits the road. No matter how thorough and detailed your plan, without action it is nothing more than a theoretical exercise.

Here's a summary of what was covered:

READY SET GO
- Handling your nerves as the day to action your plan draws near
- The importance of mindset and self-belief
- Five ways to boost self confidence
- The importance of consistency

FOLLOW YOUR PLAN
- Your retirement lifestyle plan is a formal document committing you to specific actions
- Life is going to try to get in the way of you following your plan
- You need a system to avoid being side-tracked
- Eight ways to recover from distractions and retain your focus
- Creating a condensed version of your plan
- Motivation hacks

CELEBRATING SMALL WINS

- Moving to a retirement lifestyle is momentous
- Old habits will die hard
- The importance of celebrating small wins
- Catching yourself doing things right
- Seven tips to help you shift to a celebratory mindset

THE HABIT PRINCIPLE

- Understanding what habits are and why they are useful
- Habit use by dates
- Habits build confidence and skill
- People have habits, organisations have processes
- Eight steps to changing a habit

THE ENEMY WITHIN

- Self-sabotage is real
- Coping without work as a disciplinary element
- The concept of the internal force of resistance
- Resistance characteristics
- Procrastination
- The five whys tool
- The fifteen minute rule

THE ENEMY WITHOUT

- Impacts of the people around us
- Why people resist change
- Covert versus overt reactions
- Leading challenging conversations

PUSH YOUR BOUNDARIES

- We put our own limits on our success
- You are capable of much more than you think
- Taking calculated risks

SO, YOU HAVE A PLAN

- Engaging your plan through action
- Everyone's plans are different
- A plan is not a static document
- Forcing progress – one step at a time
- Steps to aid action taking
- No plan survives intact once implemented
- Failure on happens to you if you give up – everything else is a learning experience

THE COVID19 PANDEMIC

- Covid 19 opportunities
- Success stories
- Don't let uncertainty hold you back. Change is every-where – Covid19 is but one example

That's All Folks

Well, it's not really all – not for you anyhow. Whilst our journey together, through this book, has come to an end, your personal journey - to create your best retirement lifestyle - is really just beginning. The best news is – you can do this! When I was first motivated to put this book together, it was to help others achieve the sort of lifestyle where they had more control over their lives in retirement than would otherwise have been possible. I'm hoping that I have achieved that goal for you and that you are now in a far better position to move forward on turning your retirement lifestyle dream into a reality.

No matter where you are, presently, in your life – ahead of the curve or behind it – doesn't matter, because you know what? Standing in the present, your past is history, there is nothing you can do to change it – but you can learn from it. What about the future? Well, that is another matter entirely! You create your future – starting from this very day. All it takes is for you to step outside of your comfort zone, to burst that bubble that is the illusion of security (with a job) and take bold steps forward to re-engineer your life.

With this book (and the supporting website), I have provided you with everything you need to create your own blueprint for success going forward. What you now need to provide is some effort and a commitment to see your retirement lifestyle plan through. If you do that, I can guarantee you that you will be thankful that you first made the decision to buy and read this book, then put in the effort to create your retirement lifestyle plan and took action like there was no tomorrow!

The very next thing you should do (and it will be the last piece of advice I am going to provide you with here) is to head over to the website and become a part of the support community so that you can take advantage of the resources there. (www.whencaniretire.com.au).

The step after that? Well, that's up to you, isn't it?

You Can Hire Dennis Hall

Dennis is an in demand and accomplished keynote speaker, conference presenter and business development coach, with over15 years experience. He is highly regarded for his ability to turn complex topics into simple take-aways.

His unique blend of formal learning and experience delivers plenty of impact for those he presents to, trains and coaches. He regularly speaks at conferences throughout Australia and Internationally - from groups as small as 8 through to packed auditoriums of over 500 - on subjects such as; "Building better business relationships", "Generational diversity", "Personal productivity in business", "Putting customers first", "Negotiation skills" and "Digital marketing for analogue thinkers".

His current "Keynote" presentations include:

- The Six Deadly Sins of Negotiation
- Invisible Influence
- 12 Things Highly Productive People Do
- The Secret Language of Business
- Timeshifting
- The Retirement Myth

Dennis has a relaxed presentation style that audiences identify with and is able to combine worthwhile information with personal observation, delivered in ways that can really get your message across.

He can be contacted by email at dennis@dennishall.com.au

Acknowledgements

When I started putting this book together in mid 2018 I did not realise the magnitude of what I was taking on. In fact, I so underestimated the scope of this that I was certain that I would be finished by the end of that year! However, as my research led to other research which, in turn, led me to want answers to even more questions, I realised that writing this book was going to take a lot more than I could have imagined.

I certainly could not have completed the book without the support of many people. Firstly, my wife, Iris, for putting up with my ramblings and providing guidance that kept me on track and to Tony Ryan who provided me with so many insights as a published author, as well as introducing me to some great thought leaders in the retirement lifestyle space.

Then there was my small army of volunteer editors who gave of their time so willingly to read my work in progress and provide invaluable feedback – my daughter Cristal who challenged me to back up some of my more radical theories with proof, my brothers Jeff and Greg who not only provided some great insights but who gave me much encouragement. My good friend Rick Powell who challenged me to decide who I was really writing the book for.

This book would look very different– in fact, it my not have even been completed - without their input and support.

A final thank you to Ralph Anania, Rick Powell, Tony Ryan, Shawn Ket, Keith Dugdale and David Cavanagh for their glowing recommendations!

Additional Resources And Further Reading

This book's support website (www.whencaniretire.com.au) contains templates, articles, case studies and tools which are designed to assist you in successfully compiling your own, personalised, retirement lifestyle plan.

There are also a number of books that I recommend that you take a look at as they provide additional perspectives and insights that I know you will find useful.

"Thinking, Fast and Slow" published in 2011 Daniel Kahneman

"Appetite for Self-Destruction" by Steve Knopper

"The Long Tail" by Chris Anderson

Who Moved My Cheese? Book by Spencer Johnson

Our Iceberg is Melting - by Holger Rathgeber and John Kotter

David Allen – Getting Things Done

Five Day Weekend – Nik Halik & Garret B Gunderson

Escape – Anik Singal

The Element – Ken Robinson

The War of Art – Stephen Pressfield

Smarter Selling – Keith Dugdale and David Lambert

Getting to Yes – Roger Fisher

Crucial Conversations – Kerry Patterson, Joseph Grenny, et al

The Negotiation Book – Steve Gates

Failure to Communicate – Holly Weeks

The Definitive Book of Body Language – Allan and Barbara Pease

I-Disrupted – Michael Baxter and John Straw

You may also find these websites helpful:

https://www.smartinsights.com/

https://www.mindtools.com/

How-to-reprogram-your-subconscious-mind-for-success-and-happiness https://greatperformersacademy.com/habits/how-to-reprogram-your-subconscious-mind-for-success-and-happiness

Before the Music Dies https://www.youtube.com/watch?v=9RIkDljsk0s

References

SECTION ONE

Critical Thinking Model http://www.learnhigher.ac.uk/ -

Victim Mentality https://psychcentral.com/blog/the-10-warning-signs-of-having-a-victim-mentality/

Business Risk https://corporatefinanceinstitute.com/resources/knowledge/finance/business-risk/

Escape the clutches of your Comfort Zone
https://www.redbull.com/gb-en/escape-comfort-zone

Why Getting Comfortable With Discomfort Is Crucial To Success
https://www.forbes.com/sites/margiewarrell/2013/04/22/is-comfort-holding-you-back/#274fb3cc74d4

Dr Ken Dychwald "The Age Wave"
https://www.youtube.com/watch?v=FsPPlDXyPpo&t=48s

Discover your passion - kevinhogan.com

Australian Bureau of Statistics, Census of Population and Housing 2011 and 2016 https://www.abs.gov.au/census

The 50-60 Something Start-up Entrepreneur: How to Quickly Start and Run a Successful Small Business Wigglesworth, Pamela.

The population bomb http://waitbutwhy.com/2013/08/what-if-all-71-billion-people-moved-to.html)

SECTION TWO

On Death and Dying - Elizabeth Kübler-Ross

Start with Why - Simon Sinek
https://www.youtube.com/watch?v=u4ZoJKF_VuA

Creative Thinking - Edward DeBono –

Conscious Competency Frameworks
https://www.mindtools.com/pages/article/newISS_96.htm
The 24 Hour Turnaround – Jim Hartness and Neil Eskelen
Never Too Late To Start Up – Rob Komblum
SECTION THREE
Small Wins -The Power of Habit - Charles Duhigg
Do One Thing Different - William O'Hanlon
The War of Art - Steven Pressfield
In Praise of Slow – Carl Honore

www.ingramcontent.com/pod-product-compliance
Lightning Source LLC
Chambersburg PA
CBHW061149220326
41599CB00025B/4416